The
Terrible
{*Meanings*}
of
Names

Or Why You Shouldn't Poke Your Giselle with a Barry

JUSTIN CORD HAYES

Aadamsmedia
Avon, Massachussets

Published by
Adams Media, a division of F+W Media, Inc.
57 Littlefield Street, Avon, MA 02322. U.S.A.
www.adamsmedia.com

ISBN 10: 1-4405-5255-X
ISBN 13: 978-1-4405-5255-7
eISBN 10: 1-4405-5256-8
eISBN 13: 978-1-4405-5256-4

Printed in the United States of America.

10   9   8   7   6   5   4   3   2   1

This book is available at quantity discounts for bulk purchases.
For information, please call 1-800-289-0963.

Dedication

This book is dedicated to my son Parker (park keeper) and my step-daughter Abigail (my father is joy), both of whom will make names for themselves. And to my stepson Jake. His name has a terrible meaning (deceiver), but he's going to give all Jakes a good name.

Acknowledgments

Grateful acknowledgment is made to Halli Melnitsky, Katie Corcoran Lytle, and Victoria Sandbrook, all of Adams Media, for giving me the opportunity to write this book. Thanks!

CONTENTS

Introduction

Jacob. Kelly. Mary.

These all sound like great names, right? Names that are given to those who are upright, honest, and all-around good people? Guess again!

Jacob, Kelly, and Mary may sound all warm and fuzzy, but in actuality these ordinary names have pretty terrible meanings that parents would do well to avoid. Jacob means cheater. Kelly means war or strife. And Mary means bitterness or rebellion. The truth of the matter is that there are a lot of ordinary names that really just have terrible, unexpected, violent, angry, dark meanings . . . and here in *The Terrible Meanings of Names*, you'll learn what names (or people!) to avoid and what names you might actually want to consider when naming a child or pet, or even just when making a new friend.

For each ordinary name with a regrettably poor meaning, you'll learn:

- The gender of each name, or whether it's unisex
- The terrible meaning behind each seemingly innocuous name
- The origin and etymology of each name
- Variations and alternate spellings for that name
- The rank of each name based on information from the Social Security Administration's website

You'll also find groupings of similarly terrible names at the end of the book, just in case you find yourself looking for a list of Good Names for Girls with Terrible Personalities (Delilah, Emily, or Rhonda) or Good Names for the Terribly Ugly (Brad, Courtney, or Penelope). In addition, you'll also be given a chance to reconsider some names that have rotten associations (Adolph, Saddam) or that just don't sound very good to Western ears (Bertha, Helga). Some of these "bad" names actually have great meanings. Adolph, for example, means noble wolf, which evokes a strong, vigorous child. And as ugly as Bertha sounds, it means bright and famous.

So before you buy into William Shakespeare's idea that "a rose by any other name would smell as sweet," take some time to think about what that name really means. There's a good chance that it's a lot more terrible than you would have thought.

The Terrible {*Meanings*} of Ordinary Names

Chances are, you've never given much thought to the meaning of your name. But maybe you should. For that matter, you definitely should familiarize yourself with name meanings before you consider having children or give serious thought to meeting up with that guy/gal you met on Craigslist. For that matter, would you ever go on Craigslist if it were called Rockslist? Craig is Gaelic for rocks, after all.

In this section, you will learn about hundreds of names with unfortunate meanings. Names are alphabetical, and each entry includes such information as the names' popularity; famous people with those unfortunate appellations; variant spellings of the names; and the names' rotten, etymological roots. Hopefully, you won't find your own name among the following. If you're lucky, you'll just find those of backstabbing colleagues, and you can use the information included herein to embarrass them at the next staff meeting.

Addison MEANING: son of Adam

{Yeah, we really wanted a boy.}

GENDER: female | **ORIGIN:** English | **RANKING:** 13

ETYMOLOGY: Addison derives from an Old English surname meaning son of Adam. Gender issues, anyone?

VARIATIONS: Addeson, Addis, Addisen, Addisson, Addyson

FAMOUS ADDISONS: Since 2005, Kate Walsh has played Dr. Addison Montgomery, who battles disease and challenging personal issues on *Grey's Anatomy* and *Private Practice*.

Aiden MEANING: little fire

{Aiden is destined to be a little devil. It's right there in his name.}

GENDER: unisex, typically male | **ORIGIN:** Irish | **RANKING:** 9

ETYMOLOGY: This kid is smokin'! Aiden derives from Aed, a god of the underworld in Irish mythology. His name means fire, and the *en* on the end of the name means little.

VARIATIONS: Aden, Aidenn, Ayden, Aidan, Eadin

Alan MEANING: little rock

{That's what you get for being born in Arkansas!}

GENDER: male | **ORIGIN:** Irish | **RANKING:** 163

ETYMOLOGY: Alan derives from the Gaelic *ailin*, which means little rock. Pebbles can be decorative, but they can also get stuck in your shoe and annoy the crap out of you. Cute and annoying. Hmm. Just like babies.

VARIATIONS: Aland, Allan, Allen, Allyn, Alain

Alena   MEANING: torch

{Don't hang out with her, dude. You'll get burned.}

GENDER: female | **ORIGIN:** Greek | **RANKING:** 744

ETYMOLOGY: Alena is from the Greek *helene*, which means torch.

VARIATIONS: Ailina, Aleana, Aleena, Alenah, Alyna

FAMOUS ALENAS: Saint Alena was martyred in 644 c.e. and canonized in 1193. Her pagan father caused her death after learning she had become a baptized Christian. So even if you name your kid Alena, you're a better parent than that guy!

Alexia   MEANING: word blindness

{Waht this deos say? I can't raed it!}

GENDER: female | **ORIGIN:** Greek | **RANKING:** 275

ETYMOLOGY: Technically, *alexia* is Greek for defender, but it's also the technical name for acquired dyslexia, also known as word blindness, caused by a brain injury.

VARIATIONS: Aleksia, Aleska, Alessia, Alexcia, Alexea

FAMOUS ALEXIAS: Cyprus may be in economic trouble, but its pop music export, Alexia Vassilou (known simply as Alexia), continues to rack up gold and platinum records throughout Europe.

Top Names and Their Meanings for Twins: Female Edition

Twins are one out of eighty births. Often, parents choose to give their twins complementary names. Sometimes, the names rhyme or sound euphonious together. At other times, the names are complementary virtues or character traits. The top-five twin names for female twins and their meanings follow.

- Makayla and Makenzie come in at number five. Makayla is a feminine variant of Michael, which asks the rhetorical question, "Who is like God?" Makenzie means handsome.
- Faith and Hope are number four. The names are virtues many would like their children to possess.
- Ella and Emma are at number three. Ella means other, and Emma means whole or universal.
- Gabriella and Isabella rank second. Gabriella is the feminine form of Gabriel, which means strong man of God. Isabella is a form of Elizabeth and means my God is abundance.
- And ranked number one are Olivia and Sophia. Olivia means elf army, and Sophia means wisdom.

Alfonso MEANING: ready for battle

{*My therapist says I'm terrible at choosing my battles.*}

GENDER: male | ORIGIN: German | RANKING: 793

ETYMOLOGY: Children will argue throughout their lives: I want ice cream for breakfast! Can I borrow the car for the weekend? Will you give me fifty bucks for no reason at all? Why, oh why, would anyone want to add to the aggravation? Alfonso stems from the German *hadu* (battle) and *funs* (ready). He'll be itching for a fight on *every single issue.*

VARIATIONS: Alfonz, Alfonze, Alonzo, Alphons, Fonso

Alfredo MEANING: elf counsel

{*He's pretty good at his job, but he can only find solutions for* very small *problems.*}

GENDER: male | ORIGIN: English | RANKING: 483

ETYMOLOGY: Alfred sounds too old-fashioned to be truly popular. It barely scrapes the top one thousand. Add that *o* to the end, however, and you end up with a zippier name . . . *and* a tasty pasta dish! Alfredo (and Alfred) comes from the Old English *aelf* (elf) and *raed* (counsel). Elves were once considered especially beautiful, magical creatures. Why they would need counselors is unclear. Perhaps they had little bitty inferiority complexes. Or maybe their magical powers allowed them to see that, one day, elves would be associated with the commercialization of a holiday and with cookie pitchmen who live in a hollow tree.

VARIATIONS: Alfred, Fredo, Fred, Ulfried, Ulfrid

Alton   MEANING: old town

{There's gonna be a hot time in the Alton tonight!}

GENDER: male | **ORIGIN:** English | **RANKING:** not in the top 1,000
ETYMOLOGY: Alton began as a British surname for people who came from the "old town." What's the old town? That's lost to history. Chances are, though, that it was pretty boring and filled with lots of sheep.
VARIATIONS: Aldon, Alston, Alten, Allten, Elton
FAMOUS ALTONS: Alton Brown makes mouths water as the host of Food Network's *Good Eats.*

Amara   MEANING: bitter

{Is it any wonder her divorce was so acrimonious?}

GENDER: female | **ORIGIN:** Latin | **RANKING:** 587
ETYMOLOGY: Amara likely derives from the Latin *acerbus*, meaning bitter. Need I say more?
VARIATIONS: Amaira, Amairani, Amari, Amariah, Amarra
FAMOUS AMARAS: English actress Amara Karan made her screen debut in Wes Anderson's *The Darjeeling Limited.*

Amaya   MEANING: the end

{Right after Amaya was born, I couldn't get a vasectomy fast enough!}

GENDER: female | **ORIGIN:** Basque | **RANKING:** 210
ETYMOLOGY: Amaya comes from *amaia*, which is Basque for the end. The Basque people live in a region straddling France and Spain. "The end" can refer to the following: 1) The conclusion of a long and boring story. 2) Someone's butt. 3) Something really awesome.
VARIATIONS: Amaia, Amaiah, Amayah, Ammaya, Amya

What's Your Name Again?

Samuel Clemens (1835–1910) was a successful riverboat captain who liked to write. An older, officious captain wrote occasional pieces for newspapers, using the name Mark Twain. Clemens wrote a satirical piece about the captain, whose name was Isaiah Sellers. The piece supposedly hurt Sellers so much that he stopped writing. When the Civil War disrupted riverboat piloting —rivers had become corridors of war, not of commerce and transportation—Clemens moved out West. While in Nevada, he heard that Sellers had died. Clemens, still writing and not wanting to hurt the feelings of others (at least at that point in his career), adopted Sellers's pseudonym. Mark Twain is riverboat speak for "this water is two fathoms deep." Water of that depth was considered safe for passage.

Amos MEANING: burdened

{He's our little burden of joy!}

GENDER: male | **ORIGIN:** Hebrew | **RANKING:** 860
ETYMOLOGY: The biblical prophet's name translates to *carry* or *burden*. The Book of Amos is one of those biblical books that most people don't know exists. Amos spends most of his book prophesying "the Day of the Lord," i.e., Judgment Day. That's strike one against this name. The original Amos was a total downer. Strike two is due to the once popular, now embarrassing-that-it-ever-existed radio and television show *Amos 'n' Andy*, which featured stereotypical depictions of life in an African-American community. Thanks to this show, Amos was used rarely in the United States until recent years.
VARIATIONS: Ames, Amoss, Amose, Amous, Aymoss

Andrea MEANING: strong and manly

{I'm afraid she's just not Toddlers & Tiaras material.}

GENDER: female | **ORIGIN:** Greek | **RANKING:** 81
ETYMOLOGY: Tomboys of the world can unite behind this name, although even many of them won't like being described as manly. That detracts from girl power. Andrea, the female version of Andrew, stems from the Greek *andros*, which means man.
VARIATIONS: Aundria, Ohndrea, Ohndreea, Ohndria, Ondria

Aphra MEANING: dust

{Aphra to Aphra; dust to dust.}

GENDER: female | **ORIGIN:** Hebrew | **RANKING:** not in the top 1,000
ETYMOLOGY: In Hebrew, *aphra* means dust. Dust is nasty. It contains such things as small amounts of dead skin, pet hair, human hair, pol-

len, textile fibers, and paper fibers. It can spark asthma and hay fever. That's what you want as a name? Hay Fever Inducer?

VARIATIONS: Afra, Alpha, Ofra, Affery, Afraa

FAMOUS APHRAS: Aphra Behn (1640–1689) was one of the first professional female writers in English. She also served as a spy for King Charles II.

Apollo MEANING: destroyer

{ It wasn't long after he was born that we knew we'd never get our damage deposit back. }

GENDER: male | **ORIGIN:** Greek | **RANKING:** not in the top 1,000

ETYMOLOGY: Coming soon to a nursery near you! He destroys sleep! He destroys decorative items! He destroys toilets by throwing toys into them! He destroys your sex life because you're too damn tired to do anything! He's . . . Apollo! Apollo derives from the Greek *apollymi*, which means destroy. Good luck!

VARIATIONS: Apollon, Apollos, Apolo, Apolinar, Apolonio

FAMOUS APOLLOS: American speed skater Apolo Ohno has won eight medals at the Winter Olympics.

Aria MEANING: air

{ You're such an Aria head! }

GENDER: female | **ORIGIN:** Italian | **RANKING:** 157

ETYMOLOGY: Yes, an aria is a composition for solo voice and orchestra, but literally it means air. Air is ethereal and insubstantial. Air is synonymous with "nothing." That's right. Parents who've named their child Aria have basically named her Nothing. Glad she's so important to you.

VARIATIONS: Ari, Arias, Arya, Ariah, Aarya

Avery MEANING: elf ruler

{ *It's not a very big kingdom, but she rules it with an iron fist.* }

GENDER: unisex, typically female | ORIGIN: German | RANKING: 18
ETYMOLOGY: Avery began as a diminutive of the name Alberich, which is made up of two words: *alf* (elf) and *ric* (power; ruler). Even though elves are now associated with Santa, they once were considered magical creatures of exceptional beauty. Avery's namesake, Alberich, was king of the little people in Germanic mythology.
VARIATIONS: Aubrey, Aivree, Avari, Averea, Averie

Azalea MEANING: dry

{ *Hey barkeep, keep pourin' 'em. I'm a little dry over here.* }

GENDER: female | ORIGIN: Greek | RANKING: not in the top 1,000
ETYMOLOGY: From the Greek *azaleos*, meaning dry, azaleas are flowers that flourish in dry soil. If you're looking to be someone who flourishes under boring, harsh conditions, then this might be the name for you.
VARIATIONS: Azaleah, Azalee, Azalei, Azaley, Azali
FAMOUS AZALEAS: Iggy Azalea (the stage name of Amethyst Amelia Kelly) is an Australian rapper whose videos went viral on YouTube in 2011.

Albin?!?

First, Sweden brings us the depressing, damn-near-unwatchable films of Ingmar Bergman. Then it has the nerve to make snootiness a national policy that affects names. In 1982, Sweden adopted a law that forbade common folk from giving their children names associated with noble families. The law also puts the kibosh on names that the country's tax agency, which oversees this quasi-fascist policy, believes are inappropriate. Sweden's Elisabeth Hallin and Lasse Diding decided to protest the country's intrusion into their private life and attempted to name their bouncing baby boy Brfxxccxxmnpcccclllmmnprxvclmnckssqlbb11116, pronounced (naturally) Albin. Sweden balked. The couple tried to shorten their child's name to A. No dice. Denmark, Iceland, and New Zealand have similar laws to limit "odd" baby names.

Bailey   MEANING: bailiff

{I can't figure out why that girl is so arresting.}

GENDER: unisex, typically female | **ORIGIN:** English | **RANKING:** 88
ETYMOLOGY: People don't want to see a bailiff headed their way.
They're usually the bearer of bad litigious news: Congratulations, you're being sued! Yet many people choose to name their daughters (and occasionally their sons) Bailey, which derives from the Middle English *baili* and means bailiff.
VARIATIONS: Baeli, Bali, Baili, Baylea, Baillie

Barbara   MEANING: stranger

{I wish Barbara had remained a stranger.}

GENDER: female | **ORIGIN:** Greek | **RANKING:** 764
ETYMOLOGY: Barbara derives from the Greek word *barbaros*, which means foreign or stranger. Two of the best-known contemporary Barbaras are not strangers to the spotlight. Barbara Bush is wife and mother of United States presidents, and Barbra (note the slightly different spelling) Streisand is an attention-gulping actress and singer.
VARIATIONS: Barbra, Babette, Babs, Barbarella, Barbera

Mononyms, Anyone?

Some entertainers are so fabulous they are mononymous, meaning they only need one name. In some cases, that name is simply the performer's actual first name (Adele, Madonna, Ke$ha—minus the $ of course) or last name (Morrisey, Liberace). Some are neither.

- Gordon Sumner (born 1951) played in jazz and big bands while in college and during his stint as a teacher. One day, while playing a gig with the Phoenix Jazzmen, he was wearing a black and yellow, striped sweater that bandleader Gordon Solomon thought made Sumner look like a bee. Solomon called him Sting, and the name stuck.
- Irish singer-songwriter Gavin Friday became a close friend to Paul Hewson (born 1960) when the two were children. Friday thought his friend had a good voice and began to call him *Bonavox*, Latin for good voice. Ultimately, the name shifted to Bono Vox, but the U2 leader is known typically as just Bono.
- Christopher Brian Bridges (born 1977) was one of the first Dirty South rappers (i.e., rappers from the South) to achieve mainstream success. When he first arrived on the scene and was asked about his stage name, Bridges said he chose Ludacris because he considers his personality both ludicrous and ridiculous. Hard to say where that *a* comes from, though.

Barry   MEANING: pointed object

{ We gave Barry a stick and let him work things out with the neighbor's kid. }

GENDER: male | **ORIGIN:** Irish | **RANKING:** not in the top 1,000
ETYMOLOGY: Barry's a natural-born, pointy-headed cretin. Barry derives from the Gaelic *bearach*, which refers to the pointy end of a spear. He'll be funny looking, but at least he'll be a sharp guy.
VARIATIONS: Baree, Barey, Barie, Barree, Barri
FAMOUS BARRYS: Barry Manilow is a singer who is a guilty pleasure due to such hits as "Mandy" and "Copacabana (At the Copa)." Outfielder Barry Bonds's outstanding career with the Pittsburgh Pirates and San Francisco Giants has been overshadowed by his alleged involvement with steroids.

Belinda   MEANING: beautiful snake

{ I'm tired of all your hissy fits! }

GENDER: female | **ORIGIN:** German | **RANKING:** not in the top 1,000
ETYMOLOGY: The name Belinda stems from *behrt* (bright; famous; beautiful) and *lindi* (snake). Many fear snakes and find them loathsome, and that's probably not the attitude parents want others to have about their little girl. Then again, little girls can become loathsome without anyone's help.
VARIATIONS: Annabelinda, Balinda, Bindy, Lindy, Velinda
FAMOUS BELINDAS: Belinda Carlisle was singer for The Go-Go's, a popular group in the 1980s.

Benton   MEANING: town in the bent grass

{ Well, it beats town in the poison ivy. }

GENDER: male | **ORIGIN:** English | **RANKING:** 938

ETYMOLOGY: Benton began as an Old English surname meaning town in the bent grass. Bent or not, being named after grass is pretty lame. Sorry Benton.

VARIATIONS: Bentan, Bentin, Bentun, Bondon, Boynton

FAMOUS BENTONS: Thomas Hart Benton (1889–1975) was an artist who influenced abstract expressionist Jackson Pollock.

Bernadette MEANING: strong, brave bear

{If you say that again, I'll claw your eyes out!}

GENDER: female | **ORIGIN:** German | **RANKING:** not in the top 1,000

ETYMOLOGY: Most women wouldn't smile at being compared to a bear. However, if they, um, bear this name, then it's a necessary comparison. Bernadette derives from *bern* (bear) and *hard* (brave, strong).

VARIATIONS: Bena, Bernadetta, Bernarda, Bernadine, Bernharda

FAMOUS BERNADETTES: Actress Bernadette Peters, known for her stage and screen appearances, was born Bernadette Lazzara. She wanted a name that wouldn't lead to ethnic stereotyping.

Bethany MEANING: house of poverty

{We used to have a 401(k). Now we have college bills, a second mortgage, and Bethany!}

GENDER: female | **ORIGIN:** Hebrew | **RANKING:** 352

ETYMOLOGY: In this economy, why would you want to handicap your child further? Bethany was a town on the way to Jerusalem at which poverty-stricken travelers could find temporary respite during pilgrimages to the holy city. On the plus side, it's also the town believed to be the site of Christ's greatest miracle—the resurrection of Lazarus. Bethany, now the Palestinian town of al-Eizariya, remains a city of overcrowding and poverty, so I would avoid the name Eizariya too.

VARIATIONS: Bathany, Bethane, Bethanea, Bethann, Bethney

Biff   MEANING: punch

{ Biff, this is Pow and Kablam. }

GENDER: male | **ORIGIN:** English | **RANKING:** not in the top 1,000
ETYMOLOGY: You must *want* to spend several years apologizing to
other people for your pugilistic, punch-drunk adolescent. Biff is British
slang for punching or hitting. For some odd reason, it has also become a
first name. For some even odder reason, Biff has also become a generic
(and possibly ironic) name for a rich kid: Biff, this is Muffy. Muffy, Biff.
VARIATIONS: Bif, Biffe, Byf, Byff, Byffe
FAMOUS BIFFS: Major league baseball is full of Biffs. Biff Pocoroba was
a catcher for the Atlanta Braves from 1975 to 1984. Biff Schaller played
outfield for the Detroit Tigers and the Chicago White Sox in the first
decade of the twentieth century. Biff Schlitzer was a pitcher with the
Philadelphia Athletics, the Boston Red Sox, and the Buffalo Buffeds (of
the short-lived Federal League) from 1908 to 1914.

Blair   MEANING: flat piece of land

*{ If you wanted another name, you shouldn't
have been born in Kansas. }*

GENDER: unisex | **ORIGIN:** Scottish | **RANKING:** 973
ETYMOLOGY: Blair is from the Scottish *blar*, meaning plain. Plain is
just a fancy, pleasant-sounding word for a flat, undistinguished, fallow
piece of land. It's good for picnics and not much else. No one wants to
be named after a nondescript picnic spot that's home to legions of ants
and other crawling vermin.
VARIATIONS: Blaer, Blaere, Blare, Blayr, Blaire

Blaise MEANING: lisping

{ Thith thuckth! I can't even pronounth my own name!}

GENDER: unisex | **ORIGIN:** Latin | **RANKING:** 931

ETYMOLOGY: Blaise is from the Latin *blaesus,* which means lisp or stammer. On the plus side, this name will be cool to other kids once he gets into high school because it sounds like a verb related to recreational drug use. On the other hand, if anyone discovers what it actually means, Blaise will be the recipient of unkind comments by stupid kids, mostly boys.

VARIATIONS: Balazs, Biagio, Blaize, Blas, Blasius, Blaz

Boris MEANING: short

{ I'd pay for lunch, but I'm a little Boris this week. }

GENDER: male | **ORIGIN:** Turkish | **RANKING:** not in the top 1,000

ETYMOLOGY: Boris began as a Turkish name, Bogoris, believed to mean short. And as composer Randy Newman once said, "Short people got no reason to live."

VARIATIONS: Boras, Bore, Bores, Boriss, Borris

FAMOUS BORISES: The most famous Boris, Karloff, was born William Henry Pratt (1887–1969). Karloff's family thought acting was a lousy profession, so he changed his name.

Brad MEANING: broad, wide

{ *I'm not Brad, I'm big-boned!* }

GENDER: male | **ORIGIN:** English | **RANKING:** Bradley is 179. Brad is not in the top 1,000.

ETYMOLOGY: *Brad* is Old English for broad or wide. This is a good name for a kid who won't be able to fit in the tub by the time he's three. Go with Bradley instead. The "ley" on the end is from lea, or clearing. Thus, Bradley means broad clearing.

VARIATIONS: Bradford, Bradley, Brady, Bradd, Brade

FAMOUS BRADS: William Bradley Pitt is one half of tabloid favorites Brangelina.

Bram MEANING: bramble, thicket

{ *I prefer to think of my hair as a thicket, not a "rat's nest."* }

GENDER: male | **ORIGIN:** Irish | **RANKING:** not in the top 1,000

ETYMOLOGY: Bram derives from a Gaelic word that means bramble or thicket. These are bug-filled places that will scratch up your legs. Who wants to be reminded of that?

VARIATIONS: Braham, Braheim, Brahiem, Brahm, Bramdon

FAMOUS BRAMS: Irish author Abraham "Bram" Stoker sparked a thousand nightmares and a million paranormal teen romance books with 1897's *Dracula*.

Strange Names from the Bible

- Abishag can be found in 1 Kings. Abishag tended to King David in his old age before marrying David's son, Solomon, and her name means "my father strays" in Hebrew. Talk about the sins of the father being revisited . . .
- Gomer is a woman's name found in the Book of Hosea. She is Hosea's wife, and her name in Hebrew means complete. Despite being a prophet's wife, Gomer is understood to be promiscuous within her marriage.
- Phallu is the name of one of the biblical Reubens' sons. Reuben was the oldest son of Jacob and Leah. Phallu's name in Hebrew means distinguished, but it may not be the best, non-giggle-inducing choice for a person's name.
- Shammuah sounds like a performing whale, but he was one of King David's sons, and his name means "he that is heard."
- Zibiah, found in 2 Kings, was a consort of King Ahaziah of Judah and mother of King Jehoash.

Brandon MEANING: broom

{ The front porch needs sweeping?
Grab the Brandon. }

GENDER: male | **ORIGIN:** English | **RANKING:** 47
ETYMOLOGY: Brandon is from an Old English surname meaning hill covered with broom, or straw. Brooms aren't inherently evil, but most people hate chores, and witches are the beings most associated with brooms.
VARIATIONS: Brendan, Bran, Brand, Brandan, Branton
FAMOUS BRANDONS: Before being drafted by the Cleveland Browns in 2012, quarterback Brandon Weeden was a minor-league baseball pitcher.

Brant MEANING: fiery torch, sword

{ We don't need a playpen. We just let him sit
in the corner and play with matches. }

GENDER: male | **ORIGIN:** Norse | **RANKING:** not in the top 1,000
ETYMOLOGY: Angry villagers bearing fiery torches and chasing hapless monsters who can't help being what they are: that's what Brant is made of. Brant comes from the Norse *brandr*, meaning sword or fiery torch. If you're a peacenik, this is *not* the name for your future bundle of joy. The girl's name, Brenda, comes from the same source.
VARIATIONS: Brandt, Brannt, Brantley, Brantt, Branton
FAMOUS BRANTS: Businessman and art collector Peter Brant is married to supermodel Stephanie Seymour.

Brayden MEANING: salmon

{ At least Brayden will be a good swimmer . . .
especially when he's going upstream. }

GENDER: unisex | **ORIGIN:** Irish | **RANKING:** 37

ETYMOLOGY: Brayden has become an increasingly popular name in recent years, proving that most parents don't give a flying flip about the meaning of the names they choose for their future progeny. In this case, Brayden comes from the Gaelic word *bradan*, which means salmon.

VARIATIONS: Braden, Bradan, Braylen, Braedan, Bradin

Brenna MEANING: teardrop

{ *She brings tears to my eyes . . .
and not in a good way.* }

GENDER: female | **ORIGIN:** Irish | **RANKING:** 510

ETYMOLOGY: Brenna is from the Gaelic *braon*, meaning teardrop. How sad!

VARIATIONS: Branna, Brena, Brenah, Brenn, Brenne

FAMOUS BRENNAS: Actress Brenna Roth has lit up the screen in such epics as *Killer Biker Chicks* (2009) and *Hillbilly-Bob Zombie* (2009). Yes, these are real films.

Brennan MEANING: teardrop

{ *No, we are not crying because we're happy
to see you.* }

GENDER: male | **ORIGIN:** Irish | **RANKING:** 293

ETYMOLOGY: Through all sorts of etymological shifts, the Celtic element *braon*, meaning teardrop, evolved into the name Brennan. A child bearing this name is sure to give his parents a life of grief, but his sensitivity will make him a total chick magnet.

VARIATIONS: Brendan, Brenan, Brenen, Brennin, Brennon

Brock MEANING: badger

{Pay attention to me! Pay attention to me! Pay attention to me!}

GENDER: male | ORIGIN: English | RANKING: 325

ETYMOLOGY: Brock stems from the Old English *brocc*, meaning badger. While this may refer to the short-legged member of the weasel family, there's a good chance that someone named Brock won't be able to entertain himself and will spend a great deal of time badgering you while you try to talk on the phone, read a book, or catch up on all your DVRd shows.

VARIATIONS: Brockett, Brockie, Brockley, Brockman, Brockton

FAMOUS BROCKS: UFC Heavyweight Champion Brock Lesnar kicked much butt before retiring from the ring in 2011.

Brody MEANING: ditch

{At least it's not Gaelic for sewer.}

GENDER: male | ORIGIN: Irish | RANKING: 83

ETYMOLOGY: *Brody* is Gaelic for ditch. If you don't want your son to end up in one, it might be a good idea to avoid this name.

VARIATIONS: Brodee, Brodey, Brodi, Brodie, Baerde

FAMOUS BRODYS: Brody Jenner, son of Olympic champion Bruce Jenner, has foregone sports for a sparkling career in reality television.

Brogan MEANING: little shoe

{And here are our other kids: Clog, Tap, and Sensible Pump.}

GENDER: unisex | ORIGIN: Irish | RANKING: 777

ETYMOLOGY: Heavy-soled work shoes are awesome . . . for work. As a name for a child, not so much. Brogan is from a Gaelic word, *brog*, which means shoe. The *an* on the end means little. Little Sensible Work Shoe. That is not a name to inspire wonder.

VARIATIONS: Broggan, Braccan, Bracken, Brackin, Brogann

Brooklyn MEANING: broken land

{*We're naming the next one Staten Island Ferry.*}

GENDER: female | **ORIGIN:** Dutch | **RANKING:** 21

ETYMOLOGY: Ladies named for the NYC borough should know that Brooklyn derives from the Dutch *breukelen*, meaning broken land. There's nothing good about things that are broken: broken legs, broken hearts, broken promises. See a theme here?

VARIATIONS: Brooklynn, Brooklen, Brooklin, Brooklynne, Brookelyn

FAMOUS BROOKLYNS: *Sports Illustrated* swimsuit-model Brooklyn Decker is a likely reason this name has risen in popularity.

Byron MEANING: from the barns

{*As a matter of fact, I was born in a barn.*}

GENDER: male | **ORIGIN:** English | **RANKING:** 506

ETYMOLOGY: Byron derives from *byre*, an Old English word for barn or cowshed. The name evokes the Romantic poet Lord Byron, but this renowned lover was named for a place filled with farm-animal poop.

VARIATIONS: Beyren, Beyron, Biren, Biron, Byram, Byrum

Palindrome Names

A palindrome reads the same backwards as forwards. For example, "Madam, I'm Adam." Some popular names are also palindromes. Do these people know if they're coming or going? At least they have an excuse for being clueless.

- Ada is the four hundred ninety-fourth most popular name in the United States. It derives from the German word *adal*, meaning noble.
- Ana is the two hundred thirty-eighth most popular name in the United States. It derives from the Hebrew word *channah*, which means favor or grace.
- Anna is the thirty-eighth most popular name in the United States. It also derives from the Hebrew word *channah*.
- Ava is the fifth most popular name in the United States. It derives from the Hebrew word *chayah*, which means to live.
- Elle is the four hundred twelfth most popular name in the United States. It is a short form of a variety of names that begin with "El" (Eleanor, Elizabeth, Ellen, etc.).
- Eve is the five hundred forty-sixth most popular name in the United States, and it also derives from the word *chayah*.
- Hannah is the twenty-fifth most popular name in the United States. Like Ana and Anna, Hannah stems from the Hebrew word *channah*, which means favor or grace.

Cade MEANING: stout

{ *He's not fat. He's Cade.* }

GENDER: unisex | **ORIGIN:** English | **RANKING:** 347
ETYMOLOGY: Cade derives from the Old English *cade*, which means stout, round, or cask-shaped (i.e., wine barrel–shaped). In effect, Cade means "fatty, fatty two-by-four, can't get through the kitchen door." Fortunately, small children are notable for not ever teasing or bullying their peers. And if you believe that, then go ahead and use the name Cade.

VARIATIONS: Caide, Caden, Kade, Kaden, Kayden

Caleb MEANING: dog

{ *It's ruff to be so fetching.* }

GENDER: male | **ORIGIN:** Hebrew | **RANKING:** 32
ETYMOLOGY: This popular name really should be a total dog because that's what *caleb* means in Hebrew. Dogs are faithful companions, but they also have a tendency to poop and pee everywhere. Good name choice! If it makes you feel better, the biblical Caleb got his name because of his "dogged" devotion to Yahweh.

VARIATIONS: Kael, Kaleb, Caeleb, Cailob, Kayleb

Calvin MEANING: bald

{ *We've already started mixing Rogaine into his formula.* }

GENDER: male | ORIGIN: French | RANKING: 209

ETYMOLOGY: Calvin derives from the French *chauve*, which means bald, so go ahead and stock some toupees along with your purees. And before little Calvin starts preschool, make sure you've taught him all the latest comb-over techniques.

VARIATIONS: Calv, Calvan, Calven, Calvie, Calvino

FAMOUS CALVINS: Far from bald, Calvin Broadus, Jr., rocks some of the sweetest dreadlock-inspired hairstyles this side of Bob Marley. He's better known by his stage name, Snoop Dogg.

Cameron MEANING: crooked nose

{ *Cameron took up boxing so he could get some cauliflower ears to go with that nose.* }

GENDER: unisex, typically male | ORIGIN: Irish | RANKING: 53

ETYMOLOGY: Cameron is from the Gaelic *cam* (crooked) and *sron* (nose). So what? Lots of really attractive people have crooked noses, like . . . okay, maybe there aren't that many. But looks aren't everything. Stop being so shallow. Geez.

VARIATIONS: Kameron, Kamrin, Kamryn, Camero, Kamron

You Nimrod!

Playground bullies might still call somebody a "nimrod." Maybe the name continues to circulate because it sounds like "numb nuts." Anyway, Nimrod is an actual name. He was the great-grandson of Noah and the man responsible for the Tower of Babel, which, according to the Bible, created the world's diverse languages. By the fifteenth century, nimrod became a generic term for tyrant. In the twentieth century, thanks to Bugs Bunny, nimrod has come to mean idiot. On occasion, he would call his arch-nemesis, Elmer Fudd, a nimrod.

Campbell   MEANING: crooked mouth

{ *Campbell will grow up to be the perfect politician. Everything he says is crooked.* }

GENDER: unisex | **ORIGIN:** Irish | **RANKING:** 936

ETYMOLOGY: The name may sound euphonious, but someone with a crooked mouth would have trouble saying it. Campbell is formed from the Gaelic words *cam* (crooked) and *beul* (mouth). At least it's better than having a forked tongue.

VARIATIONS: Cambel, Cambell, Cambeul, Campbel, Kampbell

Carson   MEANING: marsh area

{ *So he smells and he's dirty. He's a typical teenager.* }

GENDER: unisex | **ORIGIN:** Norse | **RANKING:** 85

ETYMOLOGY: From Old Norse words *kjarr* (area) and *myrr* (marsh), Carson is up to his armpits in fetid water.

VARIATIONS: Carrson, Cars, Carsan, Carsen, Carsin

FAMOUS CARSONS: Georgia author Carson McCullers (1917–1967) is most famous for her first novel, *The Heart Is a Lonely Hunter*.

Carter   MEANING: cart driver

{ *We needed a designated driver for the family.* }

GENDER: unisex | **ORIGIN:** English | **RANKING:** 41

ETYMOLOGY: Medieval England had a habit of transforming professions into names, and Carter is an example of this. A carter was someone who drove a cart, so Carter began to be used as a surname for carters. At least Carter's parents won't have to be concerned for his safety when he steals the family car to go joyriding with his loser friends.

VARIATIONS: Cart, Cartah, Cartar, Cartyr, Karter

Popular Pet Names and Their Meanings: Cat Edition

The website Bowwow.com has ranked the top-twenty pet names for cats. Rankings are based on orders from the company's other website, pet-tags.com. The top-five names for cats follow, along with the meanings of those names.

- Sam is the fifth most popular name. Sam is short for Samuel, which means name of God.
- Smokey is the fourth most popular name for cats. Smokey is a popular name for black cats.
- Max is the third most popular name for cats. Max is short for Maximilian, which means greatest.
- Tiger is the second most popular name for cats. Clearly a tiger is a large jungle animal with stripes.
- Tigger is the most popular name for cats. Tigger is a stuffed tiger character found in A. A. Milne's *The House at Pooh Corner*.

Cash MEANING: box maker

{I don't much like the guy, but he's useful whenever I have to move to a new apartment.}

GENDER: male | **ORIGIN:** French | **RANKING:** 264

ETYMOLOGY: Cash has nothing to do with the cold, hard kind. The name derives from an Old French word, *casse*, which means box maker. Although there's nothing inherently wrong with making boxes, it sounds like a job that would suck . . . and not provide a working man much cash.

VARIATIONS: Casshe, Kasch, Caj, Cass, Cayce

Cassidy MEANING: curly haired

{I'm cool with it. My bro-fro makes me, like, three inches taller.}

GENDER: unisex | **ORIGIN:** Irish | **RANKING:** 283

ETYMOLOGY: Cassidy derives from the Gaelic *caiside*, which means curly headed. This might be okay for female Cassidys, but most guys hate having curly hair.

VARIATIONS: Casidy, Cassady, Cassedee, Kassady, Cass

FAMOUS CASSIDYS: Barry Adrian Reese is better known as the rapper Cassidy, who is as well known for his manslaughter conviction as he is for his platinum albums.

Cassius MEANING: vain

{He's so vain, he probably thinks this entry's about him.}

GENDER: male | **ORIGIN:** Latin | **RANKING:** 876

ETYMOLOGY: Children are inherently selfish; it's their job. Most grow out of it, but with a name like Cassius, you're asking for trouble. Cassius comes from the Latin *cassus*, which means empty or vain. Empty-headed and vain. He's sure to have a future as a male model.

VARIATIONS: Cass, Cassio, Cashos, Cashus, Kassius

FAMOUS CASSIUSES: The theatrically vain boxer, Muhammad Ali, was born with the name Cassius Clay. The Louisville native was named for Cassius Marcellus Clay, a nineteenth-century abolitionist from Kentucky.

Catherine   MEANING: torture

{ *Spending any amount of time with Catherine is torture . . . but I guess she can't help it.* }

GENDER: female | **ORIGIN:** Greek | **RANKING:** 161

ETYMOLOGY: After the fourth-century martyrdom of St. Catherine on a spiked wheel, now known as a Catherine Wheel, people associated her name with *katharos*, meaning pure. However, the name most likely derives instead from *aikia*, meaning torture. Both seem, unfortunately, appropriate for St. Catherine.

VARIATIONS: Katherine, Katerina, Kathryn, Kate, Katey

Cecilia   MEANING: blind

{ *Why can't you ever see my point? Oh, yeah.* }

GENDER: female | **ORIGIN:** Latin | **RANKING:** 241

ETYMOLOGY: Cecilia derives from the Latin word *caecus*, which means blind. The name has been popular for centuries thanks to Saint Cecilia, who lived during the second or third century c.e. The early Christian refused to worship Roman gods and was beheaded for her faith. She may have died a horrible death, but hey, she gets to be the patron saint of musicians and music. That's a fair tradeoff, right?

VARIATIONS: Cacelia, Cecely, Ceceley, Cecette, Celia

A Tale of Two Homers

The name Homer takes you to the lofty heights of literature or to the lowly depths of popular culture, depending on your interests.

Homer, just plain Homer, may have lived during the seventh or eighth century B.C.E. Or he may not have existed at all. Whoever he was (or wasn't), Homer is traditionally accepted as the author of two of the greatest works of literature ever created, the epics the *Iliad* and the *Odyssey*. The *Iliad* tells the story of the ten-year Trojan War, which the Trojans lost to the Greeks thanks largely to Odysseus, Greek commander and king of Ithaca. The *Odyssey* recounts the awesome obstacles that Odysseus faced during his ten-year, ultimately successful, effort to get back home after winning the Trojan War.

Homer Simpson, on the other hand, rarely achieves any success of any kind. He is patriarch of a cartoon family that has been beamed into homes since being introduced on *The Tracey Ullman Show* in 1987. During the first few seasons of *The Simpsons*, an *Ullman Show* spinoff that began in 1989, Homer's rambunctious son, Bart Simpson, was the stand-out character. Before long, however, Homer took center stage. He works for a nuclear plant at which he excels in laziness and doughnut eating. Though well meaning, Homer is loved, most likely, because he's an everyman. He's just a schlub, doing the best he can, like the rest of us. His story, unlike those produced by the other Homer, is an epic fail.

Chanel   MEANING: pipe, canal

{*What's that smell? Oh, it's Chanel.*}

GENDER: female | **ORIGIN:** French | **RANKING:** 827
ETYMOLOGY: Chanel No. 5 has symbolized the epitome of perfume
since it was introduced in 1921, but there's a reason it's called "toilet
water." The name Chanel originally was a surname given to pipe fitters
. . . in other words, folks who create sewers.
VARIATIONS: Chanele, Chanell, Chanelle, Shanelle, Shenelle

Chantal   MEANING: stone

{*It's not her fault she was born with rocks in
her head.*}

GENDER: female | **ORIGIN:** French | **RANKING:** not in the top 1,000
ETYMOLOGY: Chantal is from the Old French *cantal*, meaning stone.
Most parents probably think the word is related to *chanson*, French for
song. If only they knew . . .
VARIATIONS: Chandal, Chantai, Chantala, Chantel, Chantille
FAMOUS CHANTALS: Chantal Claret is an indie-rock singer who was
with the band Morningwood before going solo.

Chelsea   MEANING: chalk landing place

{*Hey, stop throwing school supplies!*}

GENDER: female | **ORIGIN:** English | **RANKING:** 222
ETYMOLOGY: The beautiful sound and icky meaning of this name are
like chalk and cheese. Chelsea is from the Old English *cealc hy*, a port
that received chalk shipments.
VARIATIONS: Chalsey, Chelcea, Chelsia, Kelsey, Shelsea
FAMOUS CHELSEAS: Bill and Hillary Clinton's daughter Chelsea was
named for the Joni Mitchell song "Chelsea Morning."

Penultimate Pen Name

Mary Anne Evans (1819–1880) had two reasons to adopt the pen name George Eliot. The first was that she wanted her work to be taken seriously. In those days, most female authors wrote light-hearted romances, and Evans didn't want her work lumped in with that genre. In the second place, Evans carried on a lengthy relationship with literary critic George Henry Lewis. There was one problem, though; Lewis was married to someone else. Thus, Evans wanted her personal life kept distinct from her literary life.

Cicero   MEANING: chickpea

{ *We chose Cicero because we can't pronounce*
Socrates. }

GENDER: male | **ORIGIN:** Latin | **RANKING:** not in the top 1,000
ETYMOLOGY: Cicero is from the Latin *cicer*, which means chickpea.
The chickpea is high in protein and has been cultivated for nearly 8,000
years. There are worse legumes you could name someone after. Lima or
Garbanzo, anyone?
VARIATIONS: Cero, Cedro, Cisco, Speero, Zero
FAMOUS CICEROS: The "original" Cicero was a Roman renaissance
man who lived 100 years before Christ. Marcus Tullius Cicero was
a writer, philosopher, lawyer, and politician. His "rediscovery" in the
fourteenth century marks the beginning of the Italian Renaissance. He
probably hated lima beans, too.

Claude   MEANING: crippled

{ *You are so lame, bro, and I* don't *mean*
differently abled. }

GENDER: male | **ORIGIN:** Latin | **RANKING:** not in the top 1,000
ETYMOLOGY: Claude is a diminutive of Claudius, which derives from
the Latin *claudus* and means lame or crippled. Even if you feel that
having children hobbles you and ruins your personal life, you should
not take revenge on that sweet bundle of joy by giving him this name.
That's just creepy.
VARIATIONS: Claud, Clide, Cloyd, Colt, Kaled
FAMOUS CLAUDES: Claude Monet (1840–1926) is the Impressionist
painter best known for *Water Lilies*, a series of paintings that launched
a thousand "artsy" postcards.

Coco MEANING: chocolate bean

{She'll give you acne and rot your teeth, but that's just Coco.}

GENDER: female | ORIGIN: French | RANKING: not in the top 1,000
ETYMOLOGY: As a given name, Coco began as a French surname meaning cook and later became a common nickname for such names as Nicole or Nicolette. After the cocoa bean became popular worldwide (in the seventeenth and eighteenth centuries), the name was considered an homage to the popular, sweet seeds. What's sweeter than a little baby girl? Cocoa!
VARIATIONS: Cacau, Kiko, Nico, Cori, Yoko
FAMOUS COCOS: If you don't count Conan O'Brien, who gained the nickname Coco thanks to actor Tom Hanks, the most famous Coco is Coco Chanel, the designer. Gabrielle Chanel earned her nickname when she worked as a cabaret singer. Possibly, the name is related to "coquette," or prostitute, so why would Chanel have been so proud to hang on to that particular nickname?

Coleman MEANING: charcoal burner

{All right, we need to pick up hamburger buns, beer, and Coleman.}

GENDER: male | ORIGIN: Irish | RANKING: 912
ETYMOLOGY: Coleman derives from the Gaelic word *colman*, which referred to a charcoal burner. In the seventeenth century or so, *colmen* were considered skilled laborers. Nowadays, folks will just think the boy was named after a popular brand of camping equipment.
VARIATIONS: Colman, Colum, Colm, Kolman, Columba

Colin MEANING: puppy

{The only way we can get him to do anything is to hit him with a rolled-up newspaper.}

GENDER: male | ORIGIN: Irish | RANKING: 120

ETYMOLOGY: Colin is an Anglicized version of the Gaelic name Cailean, which means puppy. Puppies are cute, but they're also known for peeing on your carpet, chewing up your important papers, and for barking all night and keeping you awake. Besides, who cares what Colin means? The name sounds like colon. Even if you really, really admire Colin Powell, four-star general and former secretary of state, anyone with this name will experience a lifetime of ridicule. In other words, Colin is the worst of both worlds. It's bad on the surface, and it doesn't even have a cool meaning.

VARIATIONS: Cailen, Cole, Colon, Collen, Kollyn

Cooper MEANING: barrel maker

{*At least we can always count on him to bring the keg!*}

GENDER: male | **ORIGIN:** English | **RANKING:** 82

ETYMOLOGY: Cooper began as a Middle English surname for a barrel maker. If you want your kid to work as a brewer, this is a great name, but if you're looking to get an accountant or attorney out of the mix, Cooper may not be the best choice. That said, Cooper will probably always be the one asked to pick up the keg when his frat hosts a party.

VARIATIONS: Coopor, Kooper, Coopir, Couper, Coop

FAMOUS COOPERS: University of Florida alum Cooper Carlisle has played guard for the Oakland Raiders since 2007.

Cordero MEANING: lamb

{*It's hard to be tough when you're named for cute, fluffy farm animals.*}

GENDER: male | **ORIGIN:** Spanish | **RANKING:** not in the top 1,000

ETYMOLOGY: Although the name is evocative of a matador, *cordero* is Spanish for lamb. Odds are, Cordero will spend the majority of his childhood proving to other boys that he's not cute or fluffy . . . or a wimp.

VARIATIONS: Cordell, Cord, Card, Corderiyo, Cordy

Cormac   MEANING: impure son

{You don't have to talk dirty to me. I can talk dirty to myself.}

GENDER: male | **ORIGIN:** Irish | **RANKING:** 59 in Ireland; not in the top 1,000 in the United States

ETYMOLOGY: The first part of Cormac comes from the Gaelic *corb*, meaning impure or defiled. The second part comes from *mac*, which means son. Since, as a future teenage boy, he'll have impure thoughts *anyway*, the name seems appropriate.

VARIATIONS: Cormack, Cormick

FAMOUS CORMACS: Talk about "impure sons." Novelist Cormac McCarthy's third novel, *Child of God*, tells the story of a murderous necrophile.

Cornelia   MEANING: horn

{I hear short, irritating bleats. It must be Cornelia!}

GENDER: female | **ORIGIN:** Latin | **RANKING:** not in the top 1,000

ETYMOLOGY: Cornelia derives from the Latin *cornu*, meaning horn. Horns are loud and often used by impatient motorists who are upset that you didn't start moving a millisecond after the light changed. Kind of guarantees that Cornelia will be an impatient pain in the neck!

VARIATIONS: Carnelia, Cornalia, Corneilla, Cornela, Cornelle

FAMOUS CORNELIAS: Cornelia Cinnilla was the first wife of Julius Caesar.

Courtney   MEANING: short nose

{We were prepared for orthodontia. But rhinoplasty?}

GENDER: unisex, typically female | **ORIGIN:** French | **RANKING:** 418

ETYMOLOGY: Courtney is formed from the marriage of two Old French words, *court* (short) and *nez* (nose). The name began as a surname given to folks with, well, short noses, and ultimately became a given name. Short noses aren't always bad. A bouncing baby girl could wind up bearing a cute, little button nose rather than a stubby pug nose.

VARIATIONS: Cordney, Cortne, Quartney, Kortnay, Kourtny

Craig   MEANING: crag, rock

{*I can't find my quarter. Will you look in some of those wrinkles on your face?*}

GENDER: male | **ORIGIN:** Irish | **RANKING:** 811

ETYMOLOGY: Calling someone's face craggy is a (sort of) nice way to say that someone has premature wrinkles . . . and lots of them, at that. A crag is a rocky cliff face, and the name Craig derives from *creag*, which means crag or great big rock. Thus, a good possibility exists that Craig will be a chubby guy with lots of wrinkles. And that's *before* puberty.

VARIATIONS: Craeg, Crag, Crage, Crai, Craige

Curtis   MEANING: short leggings

{*You know what they say about guys with short leggings . . .*}

GENDER: male | **ORIGIN:** English | **RANKING:** 438

ETYMOLOGY: Curtis stems from the Middle English *curt*, meaning short leggings. Let's be honest, no one wants to see a guy in capris.

VARIATIONS: Cortez, Courtis, Curtell, Curtiz, Curtuss

FAMOUS CURTISES: Curtis Mayfield (1942–1999) was a founding member of the Impressions before he went solo and created the immortal soundtrack for blaxploitation flick *Super Fly.*

What's in a (Company) Name?

If you frequent your local Starbucks often enough to pick up your mail there, then you probably already know the company was named after Starbuck, ill-fated first mate of the ill-fated ship *Pequod,* which was destroyed by Moby Dick in Herman Melville's classic. Why Starbucks? The company's founders were teachers and writers. They actually considered, then rejected, Pequod as its name. It's hard to imagine a Pequods on every corner. Some other company name etymologies follow:

- Aldi is a chain of low-priced grocery stores, often found in communities that can't (or won't) support a larger store. The name is a combination of founding brothers Karl and Theo ALbrecht and the word DIscount.
- Amazon.com is named for the world's largest river by volume. Founder Jeff Bezos foresaw the massive volume of sales possible when one doesn't depend on a bricks-and-mortar store. That seemed like a crazy idea in 1995.
- Sweden-based furniture giant IKEA derives from the company founder's name and birthplace: Ingvar Kamprad Elmtaryd Agunnaryd.
- Toy company Mattel is named for founders MATT Matson and ELliot Handler.
- Taco Bell is named for founder Glen Bell.
- Richard Branson named his fledgling entertainment company Virgin because he was a complete "virgin" at business when he began.
- In *Gulliver's Travels*, yahoos are repulsive human creatures. Yahoo! founders David Filo and Jerry Yang liked to refer to themselves as yahoos.

Darby   MEANING: deer town

{ It's not a big town. It's not a fun town. But, by God, it's got a lot of deer. }

GENDER: unisex | **ORIGIN:** English | **RANKING:** not in the top 1,000
ETYMOLOGY: Darby derives from the surname Derby, which denoted a person from a town in England known for its rich nightlife. Just kidding! It, apparently, is notable for deer.
VARIATIONS: Darbie, Darbey, Derby, Darb, Derbey
FAMOUS DARBYS: He hasn't created any deer characters, but cartoonist Darby Conley (born 1970) is known for a smarmy, pissed-off cat (Bucky) and a sweet but less-than-brilliant dog (Satchel). They're the main anthropomorphic characters in his daily, syndicated comic strip, *Get Fuzzy*.

Darcy   MEANING: dark

{ She just loves to watch people fall down! }

GENDER: unisex | **ORIGIN:** Irish, French | **RANKING:** not in the top 1,000
ETYMOLOGY: *Darcy* is Gaelic for dark or dark one. Thus, it's the perfect name for that mythological, tall, dark, and handsome man . . . or woman. A Darcy is not all bad . . . and not all good. Jane Austen made good use of this name's overtones and has fluttered the hearts of legions of ladies since introducing Fitzwilliam Darcy in her novel *Pride and Prejudice* . . . the one *without* zombies.
VARIATIONS: D'arcy, Darcey, Darsey, Darsy, Darci
FAMOUS DARCYS: Darci Kistler was a principal ballerina with the New York City Ballet from 1980 until her retirement in 2010. Darcy Hordichuk has been in the National Hockey League since 2000.

Darnell MEANING: grass, hidden spot

{ *Um, yeah, I stash all my "Darnell" in my sock drawer, along with Fritos, in case I get the munchies.* }

GENDER: male | ORIGIN: French, Old English | RANKING: 880
ETYMOLOGY: The name Darnell has two fathers. One is French. One is English. The French one, in addition to disliking Americans and carrying long bread that's too big for its bag, is *darnel*, which means grass. In addition to causing allergies, grass is something you have to mow unless you pay someone else to do it. The British father, known for bad food and bad teeth, is *derne*, or hidden place. What's he hiding? Why is he so secretive? What's his problem?
VARIATIONS: Darnall, Darneil, Darnel, Darn, Darnele

Deianira MEANING: husband killer

{ *We haven't lost a son. We've gained a daughter. Actually, maybe we have lost a son.* }

GENDER: female | ORIGIN: Greek | RANKING: not in the top 1,000
ETYMOLOGY: Deianira is Greek for man destroyer. The mythological Deianira sharpened her knives for a particular man. She was Hercules's third wife and killed him by giving him the Shirt of Nessus. The garment was covered in the poisoned blood of a centaur. Once he donned it, he went nuts and jumped into a fire.
VARIATIONS: Dayanara, Deyanira, Dianara, Diya, Nara
FAMOUS DEIANIRAS: Dayanara Torres Delgado of Puerto Rico was crowned Miss Universe in 1993. She has since gone on to music and screen fame in the Philipines and in her native Puerto Rico.

Deborah MEANING: bee

{ *Mess with Deb; you get the stinger.* }

GENDER: female | ORIGIN: Hebrew | RANKING: 808

ETYMOLOGY: Deborah derives from *dvora*, which means bee. The name has been popular for centuries thanks to the biblical Deborah, the only female judge of the Old Testament. However, nothing ruins a picnic like bees . . . or Deborah.

VARIATIONS: Debra, Deb, Debbee, Debera, Devorah

Deirdre   MEANING: broken hearted, sorrowful

{*We've already started putting Prozac in her formula.*}

GENDER: female | **ORIGIN:** Irish | **RANKING:** not in the top 1,000

ETYMOLOGY: The original Deirdre is part of a pre-Christian Gaelic myth. She was the most beautiful woman in Ireland, but her beauty caused nothing but trouble and bloodshed. Ultimately, she killed herself or—some versions of the myth suggest—she died of grief when the man she loved was killed out of jealousy. Bottom line: bummer name.

VARIATIONS: Deadra, Dede, Dedra, Deedra, Deedre

FAMOUS DEIRDRES: Deirdre Lovejoy played Rhonda Pearlman on the popular HBO drama *The Wire*. Deirdre Bair has written several biographies, including the National Book Award–winning *Samuel Beckett: A Biography*.

Delilah   MEANING: one who weakens

{*Five minutes with her, and I'm ready for a nap.*}

GENDER: female | **ORIGIN:** Hebrew | **RANKING:** 172

ETYMOLOGY: Delilah is an Anglicized version of a mishmash of ancient Hebrew, but the root of the name is *dal*, meaning weak. Even if you haven't been to Sunday school since your parents dragged you there kicking and screaming, you'll probably remember that the biblical Delilah weakened the powerful Samson by cutting off his hair. Despite this association, the name has become increasingly popular during the last few years.

VARIATIONS: Dalila, Delila, Lila, Lilah, Dalia

A Very Happy Unbirthday to Whom?

Charles Lutwidge Dodgson (1832–1898) was a teacher of mathematics at Christ Church, Oxford, who wrote books about his subject. On the side, Dodgson had always enjoyed writing pieces of doggerel and nonsense. Inspired by a young friend, Dodgson wrote a book starring this young lady that came to be called *Alice's Adventures in Wonderland*. Dodgson wanted to keep his creative and academic lives separate, so he adopted the pen name Lewis Carroll. Lewis is derivative of Ludovicus, the Latin form of Lutwidge, and Carroll is based on the Latin Carolus, from which Charles stems.

Demi MEANING: half

{*Something's wrong with that Demi.*
She's not all there.}

GENDER: female | **ORIGIN:** French | **RANKING:** 819

ETYMOLOGY: Demi comes from the French word of the same spelling, which means half. The only remaining question is: Half empty, or half full?

VARIATIONS: Demee, Demia, Demiana, Demie, Demey

FAMOUS DEMIS: The most famous Demi, Demi Moore (born 1962), married Ashton Kutcher (born 1978), who is roughly "demi" her age.

Denise MEANING: follower of Dionysus

{*We were considering Slutty Party Girl,*
but we decided to go with Denise.}

GENDER: female | **ORIGIN:** Greek, French | **RANKING:** 603

ETYMOLOGY: Denise is a French rendering of Dionysus. Since you probably forgot your high school English unit on mythology, you may not remember that Dionysus was the Greek god of wine, ritual madness, and ecstasy. In other words, he was the world's first party animal. He probably didn't hold down a regular job, and he likely lived in the basement rec room of Mount Olympus, where he smoked weed with his loser friends.

VARIATIONS: Danise, Daniska, Deney, Dionne, Neci

Dexter MEANING: dyer of clothes

{ *Dexter, there's absolutely no reason you have to be the stereotypical man in the gray flannel suit.*

GENDER: male | **ORIGIN:** Old English | **RANKING:** 384
ETYMOLOGY: Dexter derives from *deag ester*, an Old English term for a dyer. It was a surname before it became a given name. Dexter would have been the guy making all the swirly, psychedelic T-shirts for Lutestock, or whatever passed for music festivals in medieval England.
VARIATIONS: Dexton, Dexy, Dex, Daxter, Decker
FAMOUS DEXTERS: A famous fictional Dexter is serial killer Dexter Morgan, who "dyes" clothes with the blood of his "dying" victims.

Douglas MEANING: black water

{ *You can always tell when Douglas has been in the pool.* }

GENDER: male | **ORIGIN:** Scottish | **RANKING:** 513
ETYMOLOGY: From the Scottish words *dubh* (black) and *glais* (water), Douglas suggests water infused with toxic sludge. Associating with someone named Douglas is sure to earn you frequent visits from the Environmental Protection Agency.
VARIATIONS: Doogie, Doolie, Dougee, Dugald, Dugy

Famous Penelopes

The "original" Penelope was Odysseus's wife. Odysseus is King of Ithaca and leads the Greeks to victory against the Trojans during the Trojan War. That story is told in the *Iliad*. In its follow-up, the *Odyssey*, Odysseus faces obstacles that make his journey home take ten years. In the *Odyssey*, Penelope is besieged by suitors who believe her husband is dead and who want to marry her in order to gain Odysseus's kingdom. To thwart them, she claims she will choose one of the suitors as soon as she finishes weaving her husband's death shroud. What these freeloaders don't know is that she unravels a portion of the work each day. With this ruse, Penelope keeps the suitors at bay until Odysseus finally returns. Other famous Penelopes include:

- Penélope Cruz, an Academy Award–winning actress (Best Supporting Actress, 2008, *Vicky Cristina Barcelona*).
- Penelope Fitzgerald (1916–2000), the author of biographies and novels, including the bestselling *The Blue Flower* (1995), her last novel. It involves a romance between poet Friedrich von Hardenberg and a young woman named Sophie von Kuhn. The novel is based on the real lives of these eighteenth-century lovers.

Doyle MEANING: dark stranger

{Serial Killer just doesn't work well with our last name.}

GENDER: male | **ORIGIN:** Irish | **RANKING:** not in the top 1,000

ETYMOLOGY: Doyle is made up of two Gaelic root words, *dubh* (dark; black) and *gall* (stranger). Doyle is the perfect name for a kid who will be creepy and weird.

VARIATIONS: Doil, Doile, Dowl, Dowle, Doyal

FAMOUS DOYLES: Doyle Brunson is a two-time winner of the World Series of Poker and author of several books on poker strategy. Sir Arthur Conan Doyle (1859–1930) introduced master-detective Sherlock Holmes in *A Study in Scarlet* (1886).

Dylan MEANING: great tide

{We were afraid no one would be able to spell Tsunami.}

GENDER: unisex | **ORIGIN:** Welsh | **RANKING:** 33

ETYMOLOGY: Dylan stems from the Welsh *dy* (great) and *llanw* (tide), as in tsunami or tidal wave. Pretty sure you know that those are both pretty bad news.

VARIATIONS: Dillon, Dilan, Dylen, Dylane, Dyllan

FAMOUS DYLANS: A fatal love of alcohol helped poet Dylan Thomas (1914–1953) go not-so-gently into that good night.

Ebba MEANING: wild boar

{What's she look like? Um, she's got a really great personality, and she's not a picky eater.}

GENDER: female | **ORIGIN:** German | **RANKING:** 7 in Sweden; not ranked in the United States

ETYMOLOGY: Ebba is a very popular name in Sweden, but only God knows why. It derives from the German *eber*, which means wild boar. Except for University of Arkansas fans (they're the Razorbacks, and razorback is a North American colloquialism for wild boar), Americans find wild boars ugly and scary, what with those razor-sharp tusks and all. Apparently Swedes find these nocturnal omnivores that enjoy eating garbage attractive and feel that they are perfect symbols for their precious little *flickas* (girls).

VARIATIONS: Eb, Eba, Ebah, Ebbeah, Ebbie

Edgar MEANING: wealthy spear

{Well, it's better than Unemployed Spear.}

GENDER: male | **ORIGIN:** English | **RANKING:** 243

ETYMOLOGY: From Old English words, *ead* meaning rich and *gar* meaning spear, Edgar should be a mercenary, using weapons or muscles to get what he wants. Instead, Edgar sounds like the kid who gets beaten up for his lunch money.

VARIATIONS: Eadgar, Eadger, Edgard, Edgardo, Eadgyr

FAMOUS EDGARS: Edgar Allan Poe (1809–1849) struggled financially all his adult life, but as a critic he was very good at aiming and hitting targets with his poison pen. That's almost like throwing a spear.

ESPN and Marijuana

You love sports. You don't really want to be a dad. Your wife's biological clock is tick, tick, ticking away. So, you make a bargain. Fine, we can have a kid, but by God, we're going to name him (or her) after my network of choice. A conversation much like this must have inexorably led to the 2006 birth of D'Iberville, Mississippi's, ESPN Montana Real (named after quarterback Joe Montana). Cultural guide Flavorpill, which has editions in such cities as New York and San Francisco, uncovered little baby ESPN, but he's not alone in possessing a product name.

- University of Wisconsin, Whitewater's academic advisor bears the name Marijuana Pepsi Sawyer.
- Norwich, England, mother Linda Dagless named her baby after her favorite overhyped furniture store. Little Ikea was born in 2002.
- And finally, NFL offensive players are run down—like Pac-Man by a colorful ghost—by San Diego Charger safety, Atari Bigby.

Edith   MEANING: prosperity in war

{ *We could have called you Arms Dealer, but our last name is already so long.* }

GENDER: female | **ORIGIN:** English | **RANKING:** 771

ETYMOLOGY: Edith comes from the Old English *ead*, meaning rich, and *gyo*, which means war. If she's a fraternal twin, name your son Halliburton.

VARIATIONS: Eadith, Edithe, Edyth, Eidith, Eydith

Edwin   MEANING: wealthy friend

{ *Yeah, yeah, I know I hit you up twice this week, but I swear I'll pay you back next week.* }

GENDER: male | **ORIGIN:** Old English | **RANKING:** 235

ETYMOLOGY: Edwin is from the Old English *ead* (rich) and *wine* (friend). The moment your friends learn this, hold on to your wallet.

VARIATIONS: Eadwen, Eadwinn, Edwyn, Eduino, Edwen

FAMOUS EDWINS: Edwin "Buzz" Aldrin was the second person to set foot on the moon. Unfortunately, moon rocks won't make one wealthy.

Eli   MEANING: high

{ *Anybody else got the munchies? Why am I so paranoid?* }

GENDER: male | **ORIGIN:** Hebrew | **RANKING:** 58

ETYMOLOGY: *Eli* is Hebrew for ascend or height. In short, it's high. Unless you're looking for someone to help with the family medical marijuana business, maybe this isn't the right name to pick.

VARIATIONS: Elias, Eliezer, Elijah, Elisha, Ellis

FAMOUS ELIS: Elisha "Eli" Manning is the two-time Super Bowl–winning quarterback for the New York Giants. His older brother, Peyton, is no slouch at quarterbacking, either.

Elmo   MEANING: God's helmet

{He is essential equipment for God's long bike rides.}

GENDER: male | **ORIGIN:** German | **RANKING:** Not in the top 1,000
ETYMOLOGY: Elmo is formed by the Germanic word *helm*, meaning helmet. At least Elmo will always be safe . . .
VARIATIONS: Moe, Ermo, Helmo
FAMOUS ELMOS: The patron saint of sailors was Saint Elmo (sometimes called Erasmus). Elmo Shropshire wrote everyone's favorite/most hated Christmas classic, "Grandma Got Run Over by a Reindeer." But the most famous Elmo is undoubtedly the ticklish, red Muppet from *Sesame Street*.

Emiliano   MEANING: rival, imitator

{We don't need retirement savings. We're grooming Emiliano to be an identity thief.}

GENDER: male | **ORIGIN:** Latin | **RANKING:** 281
ETYMOLOGY: Emiliano is from the Latin *aemulus*, which means rival (or rivaling) or imitator. Now, imitation may be the sincerest form of flattery, but let's face it: nobody likes a copycat. What are you going to name the next one? Xerox?
VARIATIONS: Aymil, Emilian, Emlyn, Milla, Yemelyan

Emily   MEANING: rival

{Emily even turns cleaning the lint trap into a competition!}

GENDER: female | **ORIGIN:** Latin | **RANKING:** 6
ETYMOLOGY: Emily is from the Latin *aemulus*, meaning rival. You know what they say: Keep your friends close, and your enemies closer. She'll probably have lots of close friends!

VARIATIONS: Amalia, Amelia, Emmalyn, Emmeline, Emmy
FAMOUS EMILYS: Emily Brontë (1818–1848) is the Brontë sister who wrote *Wuthering Heights*. Emily Dickinson (1830–1886) is the poet who spent most of her life in her parents' attic.

Emmalyn MEANING: work

{ *All work and no play . . . actually makes Emmalyn pretty happy.* }

GENDER: female | **ORIGIN:** German | **RANKING:** 551
ETYMOLOGY: Now it can be told! The real reason people have children is so that they will have in-house servants. Even with inflation, allowances cost a hell of a lot less than maids and butlers. Emmalyn is from the German *amal*, which means work. Now, here's a rag and some Clorox. Get in the kitchen and live up to your name! I've got an exhausting afternoon of golf watching ahead of me.
VARIATIONS: Emaline, Emelina, Emeline, Emelyn, Emmeline
FAMOUS EMMALYNS: From March 1, 2006, until her death on July 26, 2006, Emmeline Brice was the oldest woman in the United Kingdom. The 111-year-old earned her title when the previous holder, Judy Ingamells, died on March 1. Judy was 112.

Enola MEANING: alone spelled backwards

{ *Yeah, yeah, we love you. Now, leave us the hell alone.* }

GENDER: female | **ORIGIN:** American | **RANKING:** not in the top 1,000
ETYMOLOGY: The name began to appear in the nineteenth century in the United States, thanks to the popular (at the time) 1886 novel, *Enola: or, Her Fatal Mistake*, by Mary Young Ridenbaugh. Alone is bad enough. But backwards? Are you eager to shell out major sums for future therapy sessions?

VARIATIONS: Since it's basically a made-up name, there aren't any variations.

FAMOUS ENOLAS: The best known Enola is the *Enola Gay*, the plane that dropped the world's first atom bomb. Somehow, a joke about atom bombs and loneliness seems ill advised.

Eric   MEANING: lone ruler

{*Sure, you're the ruler. You're also the only one there.*}

GENDER: male | **ORIGIN:** Norse | **RANKING:** 103

ETYMOLOGY: Eric derives from the Old Norse *einn* (lone) and *rikr* (ruler). Hey, it can be lonely at the top . . . and isn't that just what all parents want for their children?

VARIATIONS: Aeric, Arick, Aurick, Eryck, Erik

FAMOUS ERICS: Eric Clapton is considered one of the greatest guitarists ever to pick up an axe.

Erwin   MEANING: boar friend

{*Well, at least he has friends!*}

GENDER: male | **ORIGIN:** English | **RANKING:** not in the top 1,000

ETYMOLOGY: Erwin stems from Old English words *eofor* (boar) and *wine* (friend). Nothing wrong with being an animal lover . . . especially if you only care for the big, scary, tusked animals who killed Old Yeller.

VARIATIONS: Arwin, Earwen, Earwine, Irvin, Irwin

FAMOUS ERWINS: Erwin Rommel, known as the Desert Fox, was a German field marshal during World War II.

African Names with Strange Meanings

If you think North American names have some bizarre meanings, then take a look at some of these names tied to the Dark Continent.

- You'd better give Ajamu the remote control if you don't want to get your ass kicked. This African name means "he fights for what he wants."
- The first time Abeje has a mega-tantrum, her parents may be thinking, "Be careful what you wish for." This Yoruba name means "we asked for this one."
- Ellema is the perfect name for parents who own a farm. From the get-go, she'll be aware of one of her most back-breaking chores. Her name means "milking a cow."
- Keep Guban away from the stove! His name means "burnt."
- You say life sucks? You think having a baby will help? Then consider the Nigerian name Iniko, which means "born during troubled times."
- Some kids are just born bad. Most likely, Ilon will be one of them. This Igbo name means "my enemies are many."

Esau   MEANING: hairy

{It's not technically a unibrow if it grows up to your hairline.}

GENDER: male | **ORIGIN:** Hebrew | **RANKING:** not in the top 1,000

ETYMOLOGY: Esau is from the Hebrew *esaw*, which means hairy. Why isn't this name more popular? Is it because the biblical Esau sold his inheritance for a bowl of soup? Is it because his brother, Jacob, had to get hairy and smelly in order to trick his father, Isaac, into thinking that Jacob was really Esau? Or is it because a lot of women prefer men who aren't hairy? Yeah, that's probably it.

VARIATIONS: Easau, Easaw, Eesau, Esauw, Esaw

FAMOUS ESAUS: If it's any consolation, the biblical Esau wound up becoming really rich and powerful, despite being smelly, hairy, and stupid.

F & G

Fabian   MEANING: bean grower

*{He may get chicks, but he can't grow beans . . .
oh wait, maybe he can.}*

GENDER: male | **ORIGIN:** Latin | **RANKING:** 291
ETYMOLOGY: Fabian has a beautiful sound to it, which helps explain
the name's popularity. Yet, saddling a boy with this one associates him
forever with limas and garbanzos. Except for the coffee variety, pretty
much everyone hates beans.
VARIATIONS: Faybion, Faybionn, Fabbiano, Faberto, Fabio

Fatima   MEANING: to abstain

{I practically invented "just say no."}

GENDER: female | **ORIGIN:** Arabic | **RANKING:** 281
ETYMOLOGY: Fatima stems from *fatimah*, Arabic for abstain. Doesn't
she sound like loads of fun?
VARIATIONS: Fahimah, Fateam, Fateama, Fateema, Fatime
FAMOUS FATIMAS: Ironically, in light of her name's meaning, Fatima
was the only daughter of the prophet Mohammed to have children.

Fay MEANING: fairy, elf

{Say that again, and I'll bite your kneecaps!}

GENDER: female | **ORIGIN:** English | **RANKING:** not in the top 1,000
ETYMOLOGY: Derived from the word *faie* (fairy), Fay is, in short—as in really, really, little people–type short—not the most auspicious name . . . unless you want all your co-workers to give you the nickname, Tinker Bell.
VARIATIONS: Fai, Faye, Fey, Phae, Febe
FAMOUS FAYS: Fay Wray got carried around by a giant gorilla in 1933's *King Kong*. Faye Dunaway was nominated for an Oscar for *Bonnie and Clyde* but lost. She did, however, get a Razzie for worst actress for her performance as Joan Crawford in 1981's *Mommie Dearest*.

Fenton MEANING: marsh town

{My ancestors weren't very bright. They built towns in marshes, and all of them sank.}

GENDER: male | **ORIGIN:** English | **RANKING:** not in the top 1,000
ETYMOLOGY: Fenton is from an Old English surname meaning marsh town. There's a good chance that Fenton won't build his house on the rock.
VARIATIONS: Fennie, Fenny, Fentan, Fenten, Finton

Ferris MEANING: rock

{We wanted a name that would capture his intelligence.}

GENDER: male | **ORIGIN:** Irish | **RANKING:** not in the top 1,000
ETYMOLOGY: Ferris derives from a Gaelic word that means rock. No wonder he couldn't get the fact that he had to go to school through his head!
VARIATIONS: Faris, Farris, Farrish, Feris, Ferrand
FAMOUS FERRISES: Bueller? Bueller? Bueller? Ferris Bueller is the eponymous, school-skipping antihero of the 1980s John Hughes classic *Ferris Bueller's Day Off*.

Top Names and Their Meanings for Twins: Male Edition

Octomoms notwithstanding, twins are the most common of multiple births. In order, perhaps, to make baby twins even cuter and more sickeningly precious, parents often give them complementary names, focusing on names with similar sounds or corresponding meanings. The top-three pairs for boys are biblical. The top-five twin names for male twins and their meanings follow.

- Ethan and Evan are the fifth most popular names for male twins. Ethan means enduring, and Evan is a form of John, which means God is gracious.
- Jayden and Jordan are ranked fourth. Jayden means thankful, and Jordan is named for the famous Jordan River. Jordan means flow down.
- Isaac and Isaiah are third. Isaac means he laughs, and Isaiah means God is salvation.
- The second most popular names for male twins are Jacob and Joshua. Jacob means cheater. Joshua means Yahweh is salvation.
- David and Daniel are at number one. David means beloved, and Daniel means God is my judge.

Filippa   MEANING: horse lover

{And we thought she was just interested in the stable boys!}

GENDER: female | **ORIGIN:** Greek | **RANKING:** not in the top 1,000
ETYMOLOGY: Filippa is from Greek words *philos* (lover) and *hippos* (horse). Being friends with horses is okay, just don't take it too far . . .
VARIATIONS: Philippa, Felipa, Filipa, Fulvia, Flavia
FAMOUS FILIPPAS: Filippa Hamilton is a Swedish-French model associated with Ralph Lauren, he of Polo fame. How appropriate!

Forbes   MEANING: field

{Don't be anywhere near Forbes in a thunderstorm!}

GENDER: male | **ORIGIN:** Irish | **RANKING:** not in the top 1,000
ETYMOLOGY: Forbes is from a Gaelic word spelled the same that means field, something that causes hay fever or requires back-breaking work (or both).
VARIATIONS: Forb, Forba, Forbe, Forbs
FAMOUS FORBES: Steve Forbes is editor-in-chief of *Forbes* magazine and was twice a Republican candidate for president (1996 and 2000).

Fulton   MEANING: bird-catcher's town

{Fulton was the first on our block to get avian flu!}

GENDER: male | **ORIGIN:** English | **RANKING:** not in the top 1,000
ETYMOLOGY: Fulton is a surname taken from a place name meaning bird-catcher's town. Keep your eye on Fulton; he's been known to fly the coop!
VARIATIONS: Fugeltan, Fugelten, Fulatan, Fulaton, Fulten

FAMOUS FULTONS: Robert Fulton (1765–1815) developed the first commercially successful steamboat, and, thanks to a commission from Napoleon, he also created the first practical submarine.

Garrett MEANING: rules with a spear

{We felt it had a harder edge than Rules with Frivolous Lawsuits.}

GENDER: male | **ORIGIN:** German | **RANKING:** 190

ETYMOLOGY: Garrett is a popular form of the name Gerald or Gerard. The name comes from two Old German words, *ger* (spear) and *wald* (rule). So, you're basically naming him Bully or Creepy Dude Who Wears a Gun Into a Bar Because It's His By-God Right under the Second Amendment.

VARIATIONS: Garrard, Garrat, Garratt, Jerrard, Jerrot

Garrick MEANING: spear power

{Talk softly and keep a big, sharp, pointy stick.}

GENDER: male | **ORIGIN:** German | **RANKING:** not in the top 1,000

ETYMOLOGY: From the German *ger* (spear) and *ric* (power), Garrick doesn't need to rule with an iron fist. He just keeps his fist around some iron.

VARIATIONS: Garek, Garic, Garrek, Garyck, Garric

FAMOUS GARRICKS: Garrick Utley is a TV journalist who first earned renown for his onsite reporting of the Vietnam War.

Native American Names with Strange Meanings

Native American names often are passed down from elders of a tribe, and the names often are descriptive of an ancestor's character traits or observations about that ancestor. As a result, the names often can seem quite unusual to non-Natives.

- How the original Arketah made it through life is a mystery. This unisex name, associated with the Otoe tribe, means "no liver."
- Alkas must have been a scaredy-cat. This Coos name means "she is afraid."
- Chato may need to see a plastic surgeon. This Apache boy's name means "flat nosed."
- Give Hokaratcha a bath . . . stat! This unisex Chinook name means "pole cat," i.e., skunk.
- Uh oh, looks like we've got a devil baby! The Sioux boy's name Tohkieto means "son with horns."
- Shut up already, Yaholo. Just because your name means "he who yells" doesn't mean we want to listen to you all day!
- What did the original Yanisin do that was so shameful? This Navajo name means "ashamed."

George MEANING: farmer

{What's that on your shoes, George?}

GENDER: male | **ORIGIN:** Greek | **RANKING:** 165

ETYMOLOGY: George stems from the Greek *georgos*, meaning farmer or earth worker. There's nothing wrong with a little manual labor . . . until you throw your back out and end up in the unemployment line.

VARIATIONS: Georas, Geordi, Gorka, Joren, Jorge

FAMOUS GEORGES: George has been the name of three presidents: Washington, Herbert Walker Bush, and the other one . . . What's his name again?

Gideon MEANING: feller of trees

{I didn't hear you. Can you axe me that again?}

GENDER: male | **ORIGIN:** Hebrew | **RANKING:** 412

ETYMOLOGY: *Gideon* means hewer or feller of trees in Hebrew. So you don't want Gideon to care about the environment? Eh, there are other things to worry about, right?

VARIATIONS: Gedeon, Gedon, Gidea, Gidion, Gydeon

FAMOUS GIDEONS: In the Book of Judges, Gideon leads the Israelites and delivers a butt-whuppin' to the idol-worshiping Midianites. In addition, Clarence Earl Gideon was at the center of *Gideon v. Wainwright*, the Supreme Court case that requires the court to supply indigent defendants with free legal counsel.

Gidget MEANING: contraction of girl and midget

{*We considered the name Gittleperson, but we thought it was just too silly.*}

GENDER: female | **ORIGIN:** American | **RANKING:** not in the top 1,000
ETYMOLOGY: Frederick Kohner created the name for his 1957 novel, *Gidget: The Little Girl with Big Ideas*. Sally Field made Gidget popular on the small screen. And yes, people actually name their daughters Gidget.
VARIATIONS: Not so much.
FAMOUS GIDGETS: *¡Yo quiero Gidget!* Gidget Chipperton is the name of a Chihuahua who starred in a series of popular commercials for Taco Bell.

Giles MEANING: young goat

{*Damn, Giles, take a shower, and stop eating the crumbs from the shag carpeting.*}

GENDER: male | **ORIGIN:** Greek | **RANKING:** not in the top 1,000
ETYMOLOGY: The name Giles sounds strong and sturdy, but it comes from the Greek word *aidigion*, which means goat or goat skin. Face it. Goats don't have a good rep. They eat tin cans. They smell. They were responsible for "Goat Boy," a particularly annoying, recurring *Saturday Night Live* skit from the 1990s.
VARIATIONS: Gylles, Gyllis, Jyles, Gilles, Gyles
FAMOUS GILESES: Giles Corey (1611–1692) was one of the victims of the infamous Salem Witch Trials of 1692. He was pressed to death after being convicted of wizardry. Being pressed meant a board was placed on top of him, to which stones were added until his body caved in.

What's Behind That Curtain?

Most children still watch (or are forced to watch) the 1939 film, *The Wizard of Oz*. The wizard is a meek little man who hides behind a frightening cult of personality. Land of Oz creator L. Frank Baum supposedly came up with Oz when he looked at his filing cabinet. One drawer was labeled A–N and another was labeled O–Z. However, Oz predates Baum by thousands of years. It means strength in Hebrew and has been used as a name—typically a place name—since biblical times.

Giselle   MEANING: hostage

{*Take my daughter . . . please!*}

GENDER: female | **ORIGIN:** German | **RANKING:** 152
ETYMOLOGY: Giselle began as the German *gisil*, which means pledge
or hostage. During medieval times, kingdoms sometimes switched
daughters. King Wienerschnitzel, for example, would raise King
Schaadenfreude's daughter, and vice versa. The idea was that pledging
the safety of another king's daughter would maintain peace. Considering
the course of German history, this plan did not work very well.
VARIATIONS: Ghisele, Giesell, Giselda, Gysell, Jiselle

Gladys   MEANING: country

{*Ain't nothin' better than pickup trucks, guns,
liquor, and spreadin' rumors in church on
Sunday mornin'.*}

GENDER: female | **ORIGIN:** Welsh | **RANKING:** not in the top 1,000
ETYMOLOGY: The country is fine if you like solitude and loathe such
amenities as convenient shopping and cultural opportunities. If you
want a daughter who will grow up to be cosmopolitan and urbane, then
you should avoid Gladys, which comes from the Welsh *gwlad*. It means
country, as in not the city.
VARIATIONS: Gladdea, Gladdis, Gladdys, Gladi, Gwladys
FAMOUS GLADYSES: Gladys Presley (1912–1958) was Elvis Presley's
beloved mother. Gladys Knight, along with the Pips, made "Midnight
Train to Georgia" a number-one hit in 1973.

Grover MEANING: grove of trees

{It's hard to see the Grover for the trees.}

GENDER: male | **ORIGIN:** English | **RANKING:** not in the top 1,000
ETYMOLOGY: Grover derives from the Old English *graf*, which means grove of trees. Little Grover will probably grow up to be a tree-hugger who wears tie-dye and smells like patchouli. Not that there's anything wrong with that . . .
VARIATIONS: Grafere, Grovar, Grovir, Grovor, Grovur
FAMOUS GROVERS: Grover Cleveland (1837–1908) was the only president to serve two nonconsecutive terms. Thus, he is both the twenty-second and twenty-fourth president of the United States.

Guadalupe MEANING: river of black gravel

{Who knows why the gravel's black?}

GENDER: female | **ORIGIN:** Arabic | **RANKING:** 353
ETYMOLOGY: Guadalupe is from an Arabic word that means river of black gravel. Nothing like being named after a sunken highway.
VARIATIONS: Godalupe, Guadlupe, Guadulupe, Gwadalupe, Lupeta
FAMOUS GUADALUPES: In 1531, Our Lady of Guadalupe, an epithet for Christ's mother, appeared to a Mexican peasant named Juan Diego near a Spanish convent on the banks of the Guadalupe River. She has long been a symbol of Mexico.

Hailey MEANING: hay meadow

{She was born with a silver asthma inhaler in her mouth.}

GENDER: female | **ORIGIN:** English | **RANKING:** 32
ETYMOLOGY: Hailey derives from the Old English *heg* (hay) and *ley* (meadow). Hay meadows are idyllic spots covered in festive wildflowers. They're also covered in cow patties and release allergens that ruin the bronchial tubes of everyone in the region.
VARIATIONS: Haeli, Haelli, Hailee, Hayley, Haylie
FAMOUS HAILEYS: Hailey and its variant spellings used to be considered appropriate for girls and for boys. It became almost exclusively a girl's name after actress Hayley Mills of *The Parent Trap* became well known.

Hamilton MEANING: crooked hill

{His original name was Politician Hill.}

GENDER: male | **ORIGIN:** English | **RANKING:** not in the top 1,000
ETYMOLOGY: An Old English place name meaning crooked hill gave rise to the name Hamilton.
VARIATIONS: Hamel, Hamell, Hamelston, Hamilstun, Hamiltyn
FAMOUS HAMILTONS: Hamilton is a very common surname but not a very common first name. One example is Hamilton Jordan, who was President Jimmy Carter's chief of staff, but that's fudging because (William) Jordan went by his middle name.

What's Your Number, Baby?

Parents with legions of children are so uncommon today that they earn their own reality shows. Prior to the twentieth century, however, large families were common. For one thing, childhood diseases were much deadlier, so parents had a whole lot of children . . . you know, just in case. For another, the world used to be more agrarian, and large broods were very useful for completing multitudinous farm chores. Thus, numerical names were pretty common so parents could keep track of which kid was doing what. After all, Five is a lot easier to remember than Susan, right?

- Oona, though of Irish roots, grew initially from *unus*, the Latin word for one.
- Tertius means third in Latin.
- Quentin means fifth, and it is the most popular number-derived name. It is ranked 408. Quintessa is another name that means five.
- Sextus means sixth. While a common name in ancient Rome, it never gained much traction elsewhere.
- Septimus means seventh. One character in the world of J. K. Rowling's *Harry Potter* series is Septimus Weasley.
- Octavia and Octavio represent the number eight.
- Nona is nine.
- And finally, Decima and Decimus are rarely used names meaning ten or tenth.

Hayden MEANING: heathen

{*She vomits on priests, and her head spins around. You know, it's just Hayden.*}

GENDER: unisex | ORIGIN: German | RANKING: 90
ETYMOLOGY: Sure, she looks sweet and innocent right now. Don't be fooled! Hayden comes from the German *heiden*, which means heathen. Devil baby! Aaaaaaaaahhhhh!
VARIATIONS: Haden, Hadyn, Haeden, Haydan, Heydon

Herschel MEANING: deer

{*Stop staring at me like a Herschel in headlights.*}

GENDER: male | ORIGIN: Yiddish | RANKING: not in the top 1,000
ETYMOLOGY: The name means deer in Yiddish. Sure, deer are cute, beloved woodland creatures, but according to State Farm, they also cause 1.5 million car accidents each year. Don't name someone after a traffic hazard . . . even a cute one.
VARIATIONS: Hershel, Hirshel, Herchel, Harshal, Harshul
FAMOUS HERSCHELS: Not all Herschels are deer in the headlights. Heisman Trophy–winner Herschel Walker is considered one of the best college football players in history. The running back rushed for well over a thousand yards in 1980, 1981, and 1982, before he turned professional.

Holden MEANING: deep valley

{*We always knew he'd live in the bowels of the Earth.*}

GENDER: male | ORIGIN: English | RANKING: 299
ETYMOLOGY: *Holden* is an Old English word that means deep valley, the perfect spot to create a trash dump.

VARIATIONS: Holdan, Holdin, Holdon, Holdun, Holdyn

FAMOUS HOLDENS: Holden Caulfield has been a favorite antihero of literate teens since he appeared as the protagonist of J. D. Salinger's *The Catcher in the Rye* (1951).

Homer MEANING: hostage

{ *The kidnappers are asking for a thousand cases of Duff Beer.* }

GENDER: male | ORIGIN: Greek | RANKING: not in the top 1,000

ETYMOLOGY: Homer is derived from *homeros*, the Greek word for hostage. All too often, hostages wind up dead.

VARIATIONS: Hamar, Halmar, Hamir, Hamor, Omero

Horton MEANING: horrible town

{ *At least we're not Detroit.* }

GENDER: male | ORIGIN: English | RANKING: not in the top 1,000

ETYMOLOGY: Horton is from the Old English word *horr*, which means horrible or ravine. The "horrible town" in question is lost to history. Is there a Cleveland in England?

VARIATIONS: Harden, Hardwenn, Hardwen, Hardwin, Hartun

FAMOUS HORTONS: Horton is much more common as a surname than a first name. The most famous Horton is a fictional elephant, created by Dr. Seuss, who helps the tiny Whos out of a jam.

Ichabod   MEANING: no glory

{ I hate to say it, but you don't have any guts either. }

GENDER: male | **ORIGIN:** Hebrew | **RANKING:** not in the top 1,000

ETYMOLOGY: In addition to being an ugly-sounding name, Ichabod basically means loser, doofus, dork, failure, cretin, outcast, etc. *Ichabod* is Hebrew for no glory.

VARIATIONS: Icabod, Icavod, Icha, Ickabod, Ikabod

FAMOUS ICHABODS: Colonel Ichabod Crane fought for the United States during the War of 1812 as well as the Black Hawk War, in which future president Abraham Lincoln gained his only pre–Civil War military experience. Author Washington Irving knew Colonel Crane, so he likely borrowed the man's name for the loser protagonist of "The Legend of Sleepy Hollow," even though Colonel Crane was (as far as anyone knows) not a loser.

Iliana   MEANING: Trojan

{ You're not getting with me until you wrap an Ileana around that sucker. }

GENDER: female | **ORIGIN:** Greek | **RANKING:** 696

ETYMOLOGY: *Ileana* is Greek for "of Troy." The Trojans were the losers of the Trojan War, but their walls were strong and impenetrable, making them a good choice for a condom name, but not necessarily the name of your daughter.

VARIATIONS: Ileana, Eliana, Ilene, Ilenia, Illeana

FAMOUS ILIANAS: Actress Illeana (yes, it's a slightly different spelling) Douglas is the granddaughter of actor Melvyn Douglas.

Innes MEANING: one strength

{*I have one strength . . . unfortunately, it's the ability to be really, really lazy.*}

GENDER: unisex | **ORIGIN:** Irish | **RANKING:** not in the top 1,000
ETYMOLOGY: Innes is an Anglicized version of Aonghus, which derives from the Gaelic words *oen* (one) and *gus* (strength). This is great if your one strength is, say, mathematical ability but not so much if it's the ability to lounge around all day in your pajamas.
VARIATIONS: Inness, Ignace, Inge, Innis, Enosh
FAMOUS INNESES: Innes Lloyd (1925–1991) was a longtime producer with Britain's BBC. He is best known for his 1960s production work on the popular *Doctor Who* series.

Israel MEANING: fought with God

{*I fought the Lord, and the Lord won.*}

GENDER: male | **ORIGIN:** Hebrew | **RANKING:** 221
ETYMOLOGY: *Yisra'el* means wrestled or fought with God. God Himself changed the name of the biblical Jacob (see following) to Israel after Jacob fought with an angel. The Bible does not explain why Jacob/Israel fights with an angel, but please don't try this activity at home. Besides, anyone willing to fight with God won't have any compunction about kicking your scrawny butt for some assumed insult.
VARIATIONS: Izrael, Izreal, Isreal, Issy, Israeli

Jacob   MEANING: supplanter, cheater

{ We were going to name him Politician, but settled for Jacob instead. }

GENDER: male | **ORIGIN:** Hebrew | **RANKING:** 1

ETYMOLOGY: The name of the Hebrew patriarch comes from the circumstances surrounding his birth. Jacob, Isaac's son, was born after his older twin, Esau, which meant that Esau would rightly inherit his father's estate upon Isaac's death. In order to get his father's inheritance, Jacob cheated Esau. Of course, all he had to do to cheat him was exchange Esau's birthright for a bowl of soup. Thus, Jacob is a cheater. Sure it's morally wrong, but just think of all the scholarship money Jacob could get with an unusually high SAT score . . . if you catch my drift.

VARIATIONS: Jakob, Kobe, Iago, Jacoby, Jakeb

James   MEANING: one who supplants

{ We're really hoping he'll become a CEO for Bain Capital. }

GENDER: male | **ORIGIN:** English, Latin | **RANKING:** 17

ETYMOLOGY: James is an English version of Iacomus, a Latin version of Jacob. Jacob arranged to steal his inheritance from his brother Esau. So, James may not be the most honest person, but at least he's not an idiot. All Jacob had to do to get his inheritance was tempt Esau with a bowl of soup. I hope it was at least lobster bisque and not just tomato.

VARIATIONS: Jacques, Jaime, Jameson, Seamus, Jay

Jarvis MEANING: spear

{*Despite your name, you're not the sharpest tool in the shed.*}

GENDER: male | **ORIGIN:** German, Old English | **RANKING:** not in the top 1,000

ETYMOLOGY: Jarvis derives from *ger*, or spear. In the late 1980s, this name was in the top 400. It has since dropped precipitously. Hmm. Maybe folks decided they didn't want to name their child after a pointy stick hurled by Neanderthals.

VARIATIONS: Jaravis, Jarvaris, Javari, Jervis, Gervaise

FAMOUS JARVISES: Jarvis Cocker (no relation to Joe Cocker) was the frontman for popular mid-90s Britpop band Pulp.

Jennifer MEANING: white ghost

{*Aren't all ghosts white?*}

GENDER: female | **ORIGIN:** Welsh | **RANKING:** 134

ETYMOLOGY: Jennifer is a variation of Guinevere, which derives from the Welsh *gwenhwyfar*, or white ghost. Though a pretty and quite popular name, it suggests that Jennifer is insubstantial. Don't rush things; let her turn out that way on her own.

VARIATIONS: Genever, Jenara, Jenna, Jennilyn, Jenibelle

The Terrible Meanings of Ordinary Names

Common Names with a Literary Bent

Veruca is a bizarre name invented by an author. She's a character in Roald Dahl's *Charlie and the Chocolate Factory*. But other, very common, names also have their origins in literature.

- Jessica has the most illustrious pedigree because it can be traced back to William Shakespeare. Jessica is Shylock's daughter in *The Merchant of Venice*.
- Vanessa owes its existence to Jonathan Swift, author of *Gulliver's Travels*. Swift invented the name for his 1713 poem, "Cadenus and Vanessa." Cadenus is based on Swift, and Vanessa is based on his lover or friend (biographers disagree), Esther Vanhomrigh.
- Sir Philip Sidney invented the name Pamela for his epic sixteenth-century prose work, *The Countess of Pembroke's Arcadia*.
- And finally, Fiona was created by Scottish poet James Macpherson. She appears in the cycle of *Ossian* poems, which Macpherson claimed he translated from older sources but were probably written by him in the late eighteenth century. You can sound smart and tell everyone you got the name Fiona from this source. Don't worry. You'll get away with it. No one else has read them either.

Jessica MEANING: he sees

{Gender confusion? What gender confusion?}

GENDER: female | **ORIGIN:** Shakespeare, Hebrew | **RANKING:** 120
ETYMOLOGY: The name Jessica first appears in Shakespeare's *The Merchant of Venice*. The Bard probably borrowed it from the Hebrew Iscah, who was the biblical Abraham's niece . . . or was she a nephew?
VARIATIONS: Jassica, Jessalyn, Jessalynn, Jessicia, Jessie
FAMOUS JESSICAS: Jessica McClure didn't have to wait long for her fifteen minutes of fame. At just eighteen months, she fell into a well. Fifty-eight hours—and a firestorm of media attention—later, Baby Jessica was rescued.

Jezebel MEANING: impure

{I'm not bad. I'm just named that way.}

GENDER: female | **ORIGIN:** Hebrew | **RANKING:** not in the top 1,000
ETYMOLOGY: Jezebel derives from the Hebrew *Izevel*, meaning not exalted, impure, and just plain bad. The biblical Jezebel was a queen who ruled through her husband, Ahab. Ultimately, her corpse was fed to her own dogs. Since some biblical interpreters suggest that Jezebel put on makeup and her best clothes just before her death, her name has also become associated with prostitutes.
VARIATIONS: Jezabel, Jesibel, Jessabel, Jezybell, Jezzie
FAMOUS JEZEBELS: Jezebel may not be a popular name, due to its negative associations, but it's certainly popular as a song title. More than a dozen bands and artists have recorded songs titled "Jezebel." The most popular was by Frankie Laine. It rose to number two on the Billboard charts in 1951.

Jocelyn MEANING: little Goth

{ *You're never going to make the cheerleading squad with a name like that.* }

GENDER: female | **ORIGIN:** German | **RANKING:** 70
ETYMOLOGY: Goths helped destroy the Roman Empire and, during the Renaissance, gothic was a derisive name given to architecture some considered crude and artless. Finally, in the 1980s, goth became a subculture like preppies, jocks, or nerds. So parents should think twice before they give their little girl a name that evokes dark clothes, sullen attitudes, and unlistenable music.
VARIATIONS: Jacelyn, Jasleen, Joshlyn, Josslyn, Yocelin

Jubilee MEANING: ram

{ *Ewe, it's Jubilee! She stinks!* }

GENDER: female | **ORIGIN:** Hebrew | **RANKING:** not in the top 1,000
ETYMOLOGY: During biblical times, the Jubilee was a period of freedom and celebration in the Land of Israel. It was announced by blowing the shofar, a ram's horn. Thus, Jubilee derives from the Hebrew *yobhel*, which means ram. Nothing like being named after a barnyard animal to boost your self-esteem.
VARIATIONS: no variations

Kane MEANING: little battler

{ *Who's mumsy-wumsy's little battle-axe?* }

GENDER: male | **ORIGIN:** Irish | **RANKING:** 505
ETYMOLOGY: Kane stems from the Gaelic *cath*, meaning battle. Go ahead and slip some Paxil into that formula. You're going to need it.
VARIATIONS: Caen, Cahan, Kaen, Kain, Kayn
FAMOUS KANES: Actor Kane Hodder battled (with axes and other implements) countless nubile teens as Jason Voorhees in several *Friday the 13th* films.

The Terrible Meanings of Names

Karla   MEANING: man

{I enjoy being a (manly) girl!}

GENDER: female | **ORIGIN:** German | **RANKING:** 351
ETYMOLOGY: From the Germanic *karl*, meaning man. If you're looking
to name a tomboy, this is the way to go!
VARIATIONS: Carla, Kalee, Kallee, Caroline, Karleigh
FAMOUS KARLAS: Karla Bonoff is a singer-songwriter whose work has
been recorded by such better-known artists as Bonnie Raitt, Wynonna
Judd, and Linda Ronstadt.

Keisha   MEANING: tree spice

*{She's the Spice Girl who didn't make the final
cut.}*

GENDER: female | **ORIGIN:** Hebrew | **RANKING:** not in the top 1,000
ETYMOLOGY: Keisha derives from Kezia, a daughter of the biblical Job.
Kezia likely derives from cassia, a tree spice closely resembling cinna-
mon. Basically, someone named Keisha is named after bark.
VARIATIONS: Kezia, Keshia, Keshawna, Keyosha, Ke$ha
FAMOUS KEISHAS: Kesha Rose Sebert, better known as Ke$ha, hit the
top of the Billboard charts with her first album, *Animal*, which con-
tains the number-one singles "Tik Tok" and "We R Who We R."

Kelly   MEANING: war, strife

{Conflict is my middle name. No, it really is.}

GENDER: unisex | **ORIGIN:** Irish | **RANKING:** 336
ETYMOLOGY: Kelly derives from the Gaelic *ceallach*, meaning war or
strife. So put that dream of a peaceful home aside and get ready for bat-
tle. You'll be happy when Kelly goes off to college.
VARIATIONS: Kayla, Keelin, Keely, Keila, Kelda
FAMOUS KELLYS: Kelly Clarkson was the first *American Idol* winner.
Kelly Ripa is a queen of daytime television.

Vote from the Pit

Cheating, lying, and screwing around. Politicians have survived these "occupational hazards" since there have been politicians. However, James K. Polk would likely never have been elected if voters had known the meaning of his last name. Polk was the eleventh president, and he's probably best known—if he's known at all—for starting the Mexican-American War, which resulted in America gaining the desert Southwest. His last name means "from the pit." It wouldn't have looked good on a campaign poster, but at least it would have offered truth in advertising. Most believe that's where politicians come from anyway.

Kennedy MEANING: ugly head

{But from the neck down, he's hot!}

GENDER: unisex | **ORIGIN:** Irish | **RANKING:** 90

ETYMOLOGY: Kennedy is an increasingly popular name in the United States, due in part to President John F. Kennedy. Kennedy's telegenic smile helped him earn the presidency, but the name Kennedy stems from the Gaelic words *ceann* (head) and *eidigh* (ugly). President Ugly Head does not inspire confidence.

VARIATIONS: Kenadea, Kenadey, Kenady, Kenny, Kennedie

Kiana MEANING: a brand name for a type of synthetic fiber

{If she'd been a boy, we were going to name her Leisure Suit.}

GENDER: female | **ORIGIN:** DuPont (American chemical company) | **RANKING:** 628

ETYMOLOGY: DuPont developed Qiana, a type of synthetic fiber, in 1968. By the mid-1970s, Qiana was a cheesy staple of every disco in the United States. It was found principally in the bold-patterned, enormous-collared "silk" shirts men with porn stashes liked to wear when making like John Travolta (when men still wanted to make like John Travolta). Somewhere along the way, the brand name became a fairly popular girl's first name, especially among African-American families. The most popular variant of the name, however, is Kiana.

VARIATIONS: Quiana, Qiana

Kirby MEANING: church farm

{And, Father, we get all the free labor we want from the orphans entrusted to our care!}

GENDER: unisex | **ORIGIN:** English, Norse | **RANKING:** not in the top 1,000

ETYMOLOGY: Holy vegetables! Kirby was first used as a surname, borrowed from an Old Norse word that means church settlement or church farm.

VARIATIONS: Kerbee, Kerbey, Kerbi, Kerby, Kirbee

FAMOUS KIRBYS: Center fielder Kirby Puckett (1960–2006) played his entire career with the Minnesota Twins. Illness forced his retirement in 1995, and he was elected to the Baseball Hall of Fame in 2001.

Kyan   MEANING: ancient

{ *Our little boy came out of the* **womb** *an old fuddy duddy.* }

GENDER: male | **ORIGIN:** Irish | **RANKING:** 985

ETYMOLOGY: From the Gaelic *cian*, meaning ancient, Kyan is the perfect name for someone with an "old soul." He'll be bookish and look with disdain on the puerile pursuits of others in his age group. In short, he'll be fodder for every playground bully within ten miles of your home.

VARIATIONS: Cian, Keon, Kaemon, Kagan, Kaiyan

Kylie   MEANING: boomerang

{ *Every time I break up with her, she just comes right back to me!* }

GENDER: female | **ORIGIN:** Australian Aborigine | **RANKING:** 58

ETYMOLOGY: Australian Aborigines who speak the Noongar language called that funny, curved stick that returns to its hurler something that sounded to settlers like *kylie*. Curved stick. It's not a name to inspire confidence. Nonetheless, the name became popular, in part, because of Australian singer Kylie Minogue, who has been a consistent hit-maker in her native land and in England. Oddly enough, none of her songs have anything to do with boomerangs.

VARIATIONS: Kylea, Kylee, Kyleigh, Kyley, Kyli

Lainey **MEANING:** wave

{If I hear one more joke about some guy "riding" me, I'll scream!}

GENDER: female | **ORIGIN:** Estonian | **RANKING:** 534
ETYMOLOGY: *Laine* means wave in Estonian. Cowabunga?
VARIATIONS: Lane, Layn, Layne, Lanh, Laine
FAMOUS LAINES: Francesco Paolo LoVecchio (1913–2007) was better known as the less-ethnic-sounding Frankie Laine. He recorded songs in a variety of styles during his lengthy career.

Leah **MEANING:** weary

{At least she slept through the night from the beginning. The trouble now is that she sleeps all day in school, too.}

GENDER: female | **ORIGIN:** Hebrew | **RANKING:** 29
ETYMOLOGY: Leah derives from *le'ah*, a Hebrew word that means weary. Thus, Leah's the perfect name for a family filled with couch potatoes. Who needs the outside world when virtual reality is so much easier to control?
VARIATIONS: Laya, Lea, Leia, Lia, Aleah

Names of the States

Fifty states . . . and not one of them is named Bob or Sally. Washington, obviously, is named for George Washington, but what about the others? Since there are fifty, let's focus on one state from each region of the country:

- Rhode Island is from the Dutch, *roodt eylandt*, meaning "red island." The name originally belonged to the state's Aquidneck Island, a large island in the Narragansett Bay.
- Delaware was named for the Delaware River, which got its name from Lord de la Warr, an English baron who was the first governor-general of Jamestown.
- Tennessee takes its name from a Cherokee Indian village named Tanasi. Unfortunately, the meaning of *tanasi* is lost to history. Since Tanasi was a large village and a central spot for the Cherokee Nation, the name is believed to mean "meeting place."
- Michigan is the French version of an Algonquin word, *mishigami*, meaning "large water" or "large lake."
- The Dakotas, North and South, come from the Sioux word, *dakhota*, which means "ally" or "friend."
- Nevada takes its name from the Sierra Nevadas. *Nevada* is Spanish for "snow covered" (*Sierra* is Spanish for mountain.).

Leandra   MEANING: lion of a man

{*I eat girly girls for breakfast!*}

GENDER: female | **ORIGIN:** Greek | **RANKING:** not in the top 1,000
ETYMOLOGY: If parents want a sweet, demure young lady, then Leandra is not the name for them. It derives from two Greek words, *leon* and *andros*, which mean lion and man. Leandra is well suited for parents who want their daughter to have gender identity issues.
VARIATIONS: Leanda, Leandria, Leiandra, Leodora, Leona
FAMOUS LEANDRAS: Leandra Rosado (1998–2009) died tragically when her mother's friend flipped their car on the freeway. Allegedly, the driver was drunk. As a result, New York State passed a law in 2009 making it an automatic felony to drive drunk with a person age fifteen or younger in the car. The law is known as Leandra's Law.

Leland   MEANING: fallow land

{*The only thing that will grow on Leland is head lice.*}

GENDER: male | **ORIGIN:** English | **RANKING:** 329
ETYMOLOGY: Leland stems from the word *land* and from the Old English *laege*, which means fallow. Meaning uncultivated, fallow is nature's equivalent of a son who continues to live in his parents' basement long after he should be living his own, productive life. If that's the future you desire, go ahead and choose this name.
VARIATIONS: Layland, Lealand, Leighland, Lelan, Lelann

Leslie   MEANING: garden of holly

{*Nothing like being named after something just slightly toxic . . .*}

GENDER: unisex | **ORIGIN:** Irish | **RANKING:** 245
ETYMOLOGY: Leslie stems from the Gaelic words *leas* (garden) and *celyn* (holly). A garden of holly would be pretty, but it also would cut

you up like a bouncer in a bar fight.

VARIATIONS: Lee, Lesslie, Lezley, Lezlee, Lezlie

FAMOUS LESLIES: Leslie Caron is a famous French actress. Leslie Nielsen (1926–2010) was a popular comedic actor. Leslie Townes Hope (1903–2003), better known as Bob, entertained troops for generations.

Letha MEANING: oblivion

{ Talking to her is like falling into a black hole . . . except, unfortunately, there's sound. }

GENDER: female | **ORIGIN:** Greek | **RANKING:** not in the top 1,000

ETYMOLOGY: From the Old Greek word *lethe*, meaning oblivion, Lethe was one of the five rivers of Hades. Seriously though, five minutes with someone named Letha is worse than eternal death!

VARIATIONS: Ladi, Lata, Lauda, Leda, Ledah

FAMOUS LETHAS: Letha Dawson Scanzoni is editor and publisher of *Christian Feminism Today*, and her most recent book is 2005's *What God Has Joined Together: A Christian Case for Gay Marriage*.

Levi MEANING: attached

{ Well, I mean, I'm not very married. }

GENDER: male | **ORIGIN:** Hebrew | **RANKING:** 66

ETYMOLOGY: *Levi* means attached in Hebrew. The biblical Levi was the third son of Jacob and Leah and an ancestor of one of the twelve tribes of the Israelites. Chances are, this will be a guy who won't move out of his parents' basement until he's dragged kicking and screaming.

VARIATIONS: Levente, Levine, Lavi, Leavi, Levey

FAMOUS LEVIS: Levi Strauss (1829–1902) created the most famous Levis of all. His blue jeans have adorned bottoms since 1873.

Popular Pet Names and Their Meanings: Dog Edition

The Website Bowwow.com has ranked the top-twenty pet names for dogs. Rankings are based on orders from the company's other Website, pet-tags.com. The top-five names for dogs follow, along with the meanings of those names.

- Bear is the fifth most popular name for dogs. The name means, not surprisingly, bear.
- Maggie is the fourth most popular name for dogs. Maggie is a form of Margaret, which means Pearl.
- Buddy is the third most popular name for dogs. Buddy means friend who slobbers on you.
- Jake is the second most popular name for dogs. Jake is a form of John, which means Yahweh is gracious.
- Max is the most popular name for dogs. Max is short for Maximilian, which means greatest.

Lilith   MEANING: belonging to the night

{She will never be a morning person.}

GENDER: female | **ORIGIN:** Babylonian | **RANKING:** 923
ETYMOLOGY: From *lilitu*, meaning of the night, Lilith is the legendary first wife of Adam who refused to submit to the original male chauvinist. She was replaced by the more docile Eve. If parents have a baby named Lilith, they shouldn't expect to get a lot of sleep; it'll take her *forever* to sleep through the night!
VARIATIONS: Lilithe, Lillyth, Lilyth, Lilythe, Lylith
FAMOUS LILITHS: From 1997 through 1999, women (and the men dragged there by them) flocked to the Lilith Fair, a traveling music festival featuring female solo performers and bands led by women.

Linda   MEANING: weak, snake

{Don't worry. She's all hiss and no bite.}

GENDER: female | **ORIGIN:** German | **RANKING:** 592
ETYMOLOGY: Linda either comes from the German *lindi*, which means snake, or from the German *lind*, which means weak. Neither of these meanings is particularly inspiring. After all, snakes scare most people, and this one is weak to boot.
VARIATIONS: Delinda, Larinda, Lenda, Lynette, Lynn

Livia   MEANING: envious

{Don't mind Livia. She's just the jealous type.}

GENDER: female | **ORIGIN:** Latin | **RANKING:** 751
ETYMOLOGY: From the Latin *liveo*—to envy—Livia will almost surely be the jealous type. Boys will find her bewitching, and girls will love to hate her.
VARIATIONS: Liviya, Levia, Livya, Lyvia, Livvy

Lloyd   MEANING: gray

*{ **Well, pardon us.** If you'd been a girl, we were going to name you Azure or Sienna. }*

GENDER: male | **ORIGIN:** Welsh | **RANKING:** not in the top 1,000
ETYMOLOGY: From a Welsh word for gray, *llwyd*, Lloyd is the quintessential name for the man in the gray flannel suit. He'll have an average job with an average salary and an average home in an average suburb.
VARIATIONS: Loyd, Loyde, Laude, Laeth, Laethe
FAMOUS LLOYDS: Lloyd Bridges (1913–1998) was the father of actors Beau and Jeff Bridges as well as a popular actor in his own right. Lloyd Bentsen (1921–2006) was a senator and President Bill Clinton's first treasury secretary.

Logan   MEANING: hollow

*{ **For some reason, praise from Logan never feels very satisfying.** }*

GENDER: unisex | **ORIGIN:** Irish | **RANKING:** 20
ETYMOLOGY: Logan stems from the Gaelic *lag*, meaning hollow, which is how you'll feel after you interact with him.
VARIATIONS: Logane, Logun, Laeken, Lajean, Lakshmi
FAMOUS LOGANS: Logan the Orator (1723–1780) was a Cayuga Indian famous for "Logan's Lament," which criticized white settlers for their savage attacks on his people.

Lola MEANING: sorrows

{No one buzzkills better than our Delores!}

GENDER: female | **ORIGIN:** Spanish | **RANKING:** 243

ETYMOLOGY: Why would parents name their child something that means sad or moody? Because they love Jesus's mother, that's why. Lola is a diminutive of Delores, a variation of *dolores*, which is Spanish for sorrows. It comes from *Maria de los Dolores*, or Mary of the Sorrows, a common name for Christ's mother in the Spanish-speaking world.

VARIATIONS: Dolores, Dalores, Deloria, Delores, Lolita

FAMOUS LOLAS: An eponymous transvestite is the star of The Kinks's song "Lola."

Lorelei MEANING: luring rock

{It's better than Big Fat Stupid Rock.}

GENDER: female | **ORIGIN:** German | **RANKING:** 499

ETYMOLOGY: She's alluring! She rocks! But she's also deadly. Lorelei derives from the German words *lauern* (lure; lurk) and *ley* (rock). Lorelei is the name of a prominent rock on the Rhine River that has been the site of numerous accidents. These accidents gave rise to the myth of Lorelei, a siren whose beauty and singing distract sailors, causing them to run their ships aground. That's a better excuse than texting while driving.

VARIATIONS: Lauralei, Lariel, Loralie, Loreley, Lorielle

Macy   MEANING: weapon

{Don't you know there's a law in this state against carrying a concealed Macy?}

GENDER: female | **ORIGIN:** French | **RANKING:** 295

ETYMOLOGY: Macy stems from the Old French word *masse*, which means weapon. Annie Oakley aside, most women would probably rather not be associated with lethal force.

VARIATIONS: Mace, Macea, Macee, Macey, Maicy

FAMOUS MACYS: Rowland Hussey Macy (1822–1877) established the first of his famous department stores in 1858 in New York City. Macy's has sponsored a Thanksgiving Day parade since 1924.

Madden   MEANING: little dog

{Madden bit his first ankle today!}

GENDER: male | **ORIGIN:** Irish | **RANKING:** 541

ETYMOLOGY: You might as well just name your child Annoying Yappy Dog, or Chihuahua for short. Madden is the Anglicized version of an Irish surname, O'Madain, which basically means "grandchild of the hound" or, in plain English, little dog.

VARIATIONS: Madan, Maddan, Maddin, Maddon, Maddun

FAMOUS MADDENS: Former Oakland Raiders coach and color commentator John Madden is not small, but he is very annoying.

Maeve   MEANING: intoxicating

{ *When I said you're intoxicating, Maeve, I meant that you put me to sleep and make me want to throw up.* }

GENDER: female | **ORIGIN:** Irish | **RANKING:** 590
ETYMOLOGY: The original Maeve was a semilegendary Irish warrior queen who inspired the famous "Queen Mab" speech delivered by Mercutio in *Romeo and Juliet*. Shakespeare's version of the name is close to Maeve's original Irish spelling, *medbh*. Queen Mab is a fairy who, speaking of intoxicating, sounds like she was inspired by some intense acid trips.
VARIATIONS: Madhbh, Maebh, Maevi, Maevy, Maive

Malia   MEANING: calm

{ *We thought Malia was Hawaiian for Nembutal.* }

GENDER: female | **ORIGIN:** Hawaiian | **RANKING:** 314
ETYMOLOGY: From *malie*, Hawaiian for calm, Malia is too lazy to live.
VARIATIONS: Malaya, Malayaa, Malayah, Malayna, Maleah
FAMOUS MALIAS: This name has risen in popularity since 2008 because it's the name of President Barack Obama's older daughter.

Mallory   MEANING: unlucky, unhappy, unfortunate

{ *To keep her from having a lifetime of bad luck, we're going to try to nail horseshoes to her feet.* }

GENDER: female | **ORIGIN:** French | **RANKING:** 290
ETYMOLOGY: The French word from which Mallory stems is *malheure*, meaning unlucky and unfortunate. Mallory began to gain traction in the

1980s, thanks to the character Mallory Keaton on the popular sitcom *Family Ties*. Maybe parents should consider what the name means since they could be dooming their fair daughters (and their future sons-in-law) to lives lived under a cloud.

VARIATIONS: Malerie, Maliri, Mallary, Mallery, Mellory

Mara   MEANING: bitter

{ *We'll say one thing about Mara. She sure knows how to hold a grudge!* }

GENDER: female | **ORIGIN:** Hebrew | **RANKING:** 842
ETYMOLOGY: *Mara* is Hebrew for bitter. Naomi, mother-in-law of the biblical Ruth, adopted the name Mara out of grief after her husband and sons died. At least she had a good reason . . .
VARIATIONS: Amara, Mahra, Marabel, Maralinda, Marra
FAMOUS MARAS: Mara Liasson is national political correspondent for National Public Radio.

Marcia   MEANING: warlike

{ *We want Marcia to have a future in arms sales.* }

GENDER: female | **ORIGIN:** Latin | **RANKING:** not in the top 1,000
ETYMOLOGY: The name traces its roots to Mars, the Roman god of war. You don't want to be around Marcia when she gets angry.
VARIATIONS: Marsha, Marcea, Marquita, Mercia, Marcella
FAMOUS MARCIAS: Thanks to *The Brady Bunch*—still alive in syndication and on YouTube—young boys still lust after Marcia Marcia Marcia Brady.

Transplant Edition

Nearly everyone loves sports and roots for a favorite team. Most team names make some sort of sense. The Green Bay Packers, for example, pay homage to the Indian (Meat) Packing Company, which helped team-founder Curly Lambeau start the team in 1921. But when a team packs up and moves to another city, problems can arise.

- **The Utah Jazz:** Granted the team began in New Orleans, a jazz hub, but it moved to Salt Lake City in 1979. Utah is known for many things: mountains, Mormons, skiing, magic underwear. But jazz?
- **The Memphis Grizzlies:** Same song, second verse. The team began in Vancouver, which has grizzlies, but it's been in grizzly-free Memphis, Tennessee, since 2001. What's wrong with the Memphis Presleys or the Memphis R & Bs?
- **The Tennessee Oilers:** This team, on the other hand, did it right. The team was the Houston Oilers from 1960 until it relocated to Tennessee in 1997. Houston is an oil town. Memphis (where the team played until its Nashville stadium was completed) and Nashville (its current town) are not. Unlike the Utah Jazz and the Memphis Grizzlies, the stupidly named Tennessee Oilers changed their name and became the Tennessee Titans in 1999.

Marvin MEANING: marrow famous

{ This is his sister, Virelle Meningitisse. }

GENDER: male | **ORIGIN:** Welsh | **RANKING:** 468
ETYMOLOGY: This name comes from the Welsh *merfyn*, which means marrow famous. Marrow famous? Seriously? Who even knows what that means?!
VARIATIONS: Marve, Marvyn, Marvinn, Mervyn, Murven
FAMOUS MARVINS: Marvin Gaye (born Gay) was one of the greatest singers—soul or otherwise—of all time. No word on how many of those fans really just liked him for his marrow.

Mary MEANING: bitterness, rebellion

{ And we thought she'd be so sweet and innocent! }

GENDER: female | **ORIGIN:** Hebrew | **RANKING:** 112
ETYMOLOGY: Christian parents eager to name their daughter for Christ's holy mother shouldn't be too surprised if their little girl turns into a hellion. Mary comes from the Hebrew word *mirjam*, which translates to bitterness, sea of bitterness, or rebellion. She'll act like a teenager from birth . . . what a horrible thought.
VARIATIONS: Maria, Marie, Maryann, Muriel, Mariel

Matilda MEANING: mighty in battle

{ Our little girl was born a battle-axe! }

GENDER: female | **ORIGIN:** German | **RANKING:** 769
ETYMOLOGY: Matilda won't take any crap. She'll beat the snot out of the other kids—especially the boys—on the playground. She will kick butt and take names . . . even when it's not in her best interest. She'll be voted most likely to head a crooked hedge fund. Her name derives from *maht* (mighty) and *hild* (battle).
VARIATIONS: Maitilda, Metilda, Matty, Maude, Tilly

Don't Be Such a Draconian Chauvinist Maverick!

Brand names sometimes become generic terms: Xerox (photocopy), Kleenex (tissue), Band-Aid (adhesive bandage). People's names, like the following, have also lent themselves to generic terms:

- Thomas Bowdler (1754–1825) (in)famously produced a "family friendly" version of Shakespeare's works, which are still causing the Bard to spin in his grave. To this day, bowdlerize is a synonym for censor.
- Nicolas Chauvin, who may or may not actually have existed, was one of Napoleon's soldiers notable for his over-the-top jingoism. Thus, chauvinism became exaggerated patriotism. The women's movement coined the term male chauvinism, which pricks the egos of men who think they're far better than women.
- Draco was a legislator in ancient Greece whose laws were notable for being excessively harsh, so unfair and unforgiving rules or laws are now labeled as draconian.
- Massachusetts governor Elbridge Gerry (1744–1814) helped redraw voting districts to benefit his political party. One of the districts was so convoluted it resembled a salamander, and local newspapers began to call dubious redistricting gerrymandering. The term stuck.
- Samuel Maverick (1803–1870) was a signer of the Texas Declaration of Independence who took his own independence too far, according to the opinion of the state's cattle ranchers. Maverick steadfastly refused to brand his cattle, creating the possibility of ownership disputes. Other ranchers began to call unbranded, free-range cattle mavericks, and by extension, the word came to mean a person who exhibits stubborn independence.

Maya　MEANING: illusion

{Now you see her, now you don't!}

GENDER: female | **ORIGIN:** Sanskrit | **RANKING:** 64
ETYMOLOGY: Maya is made up of the words *ma* (not) and *ya* (that).
The name relates to Hindu religion. Basically, what people see around
themselves and believe is reality is simply a very small piece of the
world's truth. Therefore, all we see is *maya*, or "not that," meaning
"not all there is to the truth." The bottom line is that Maya is a name
that means "not all there."
VARIATIONS: Maaja, Maiah, Mayah, Miah, Miya

Melville　MEANING: bad town

{How did you know I was from Detroit?}

GENDER: male | **ORIGIN:** Latin | **RANKING:** not in the top 1,000
ETYMOLOGY: Melville derives from the Latin words *mala* (bad) and
ville (town). With any luck, he'll move up to a mediocre town.
VARIATIONS: Malville, Malvin, Melvile, Melvin, Melvyle
FAMOUS MELVILLES: Melville is more common as a surname than as
a given name. The most famous Melville is Herman, author of a book
many people with pretensions to the intelligentsia claim to have read,
Moby Dick (1851).

Melvin　MEANING: bad town

*{Melvin didn't come from the wrong side of
the tracks. Melvin is the wrong side of the
tracks.}*

GENDER: male | **ORIGIN:** French | **RANKING:** 622
ETYMOLOGY: Melvins have the worst of both worlds. First off, they
share a name with the adolescent act of giving one's "friend" a wedgie
in the front, i.e., yanking up his underwear so that it, um, *displaces* his

testicles. The name's etymology is equally cruddy. It comes from Latin words *mala* (bad) and *ville* (town), which mean "bad town."

VARIATIONS: Belvin, Malvin, Malvyn, Melvyn, Melville

Mina MEANING: fish

{*I'm going to the bar to trawl for Mina tonight.*}

GENDER: female | **ORIGIN:** Sanskrit | **RANKING:** 809
ETYMOLOGY: *Mina* is Sanskrit for fish. Fish can be majestic creatures, leaping up from the swirling sea. They are also known for their putrid postmortem stench and for being eaten by other sea creatures and by people. That's not to mention sharks and piranha.

VARIATIONS: Meena, Mena, Min, Minah, Minette

Moesha MEANING: drawn from the water

{*We should have just left her in there gurgling.*}

GENDER: female | **ORIGIN:** Hebrew | **RANKING:** not in the top 1,000
ETYMOLOGY: Moesha is a modern variation—and feminized form—of Moses, the biblical patriarch drawn from the water by pharaoh's daughter. Thanks no doubt to the popular sitcom of the same name starring Brandy, Moesha became an increasingly popular name for African-American girls during the 2000s. But parents, be warned. You're basically giving your child a name akin to Drowned Rat.

VARIATIONS: Moeasha, Moeesha, Moeshea, Moeysha, Myisha

Monica MEANING: monk, hermit

{*Paging Miss Anthrope, Miss Monica Anthrope!*}

GENDER: female | **ORIGIN:** Latin | **RANKING:** 406

ETYMOLOGY: Monica most likely derives from the Latin *monachus*, meaning monk or hermit. If spending all your time alone with nothing to do sounds good, then this is the name for you!

VARIATIONS: Lamonica, Monia, Monique, Mona, Moniqua

FAMOUS MONICAS: Monica Lewinsky became one of the most famous "other women" in American history after her affair with President Bill Clinton became public.

Morgan   MEANING: circling sea

{And this is her sister, Undertow.}

GENDER: unisex | **ORIGIN:** Welsh | **RANKING:** 75

ETYMOLOGY: Morgan stems from the Welsh *mor* (sea) and *cant* (circle). Circling seas are a nice name for whirlpools, the sorts of things that draw swimmers to their deaths.

VARIATIONS: Morgana, Morg, Morgaen, Morganette, Morganda

FAMOUS MORGANS: Actress Morgan Fairchild is credited with making the name Morgan, previously a male name, into a popular name for girls. Ironically, the actress, born Patsy McClenny, took the name Morgan from a comic film about an artist who goes insane.

Mortimer   MEANING: dead sea

{Acres of Stinky Dead Fish just didn't have the right ring to it.}

GENDER: male | **ORIGIN:** French | **RANKING:** not in the top 1,000

ETYMOLOGY: Mortimer is from Old French words *morte mer*, which mean dead sea. As long as his parents don't mind Mortimer wearing all black and being obsessed with all things macabre, maybe this is the way to go.

VARIATIONS: Mortimar, Mortimir, Mortimor, Mortimyr, Mortymar

FAMOUS MORTIMERS: Mortimer Zuckerman, publisher and editor of the *New York Daily News*, is worth approximately 2 billion dollars.

Myron   MEANING: perfume

{I don't care what your name means, Myron.
You have to put on deodorant!}

GENDER: male | **ORIGIN:** Aramaic | **RANKING:** not in the top 1,000

ETYMOLOGY: Myron, like Melvin (see earlier entry), is the worst of both worlds. The name sounds nerdy. That's strike one. For strike two, the name derives from *myrrh*, one of the items brought to the baby Jesus by the Magi. At one time, this tree resin, used for perfume, incense, and medicine, was considered more valuable than gold. It's not anymore, and besides the name means PERFUME. Perfume. This is not a name for which your son will thank you.

VARIATIONS: Mehran, Miran, Meron, Miron, Miryn

FAMOUS MYRONS: Myron Cope (1929–2008) was the voice of the Pittsburgh Steelers from 1970 until his retirement in 2005. Actor Myron McCormick won a 1950 Tony Award for his performance as Luther Billis in the musical *South Pacific*.

N & O

Narcissa MEANING: sleep, numbness

{ *I'd rather watch paint dry than listen to Narcissa.* }

GENDER: female | **ORIGIN:** Greek | **RANKING:** not in the top 1,000
ETYMOLOGY: Narcissa is the feminine version of Narcissus. Though rarely used today, it was a prominent name throughout the nineteenth century. Narcissus is a character from Greek mythology who was (or at least thought he was) so good looking that, when he caught sight of his reflection in the water, he was numbed into sleep (Greek: *nark*) and ultimately died. Thus, Narcissa has the potential to be both narcoleptic and narcissistic. No wonder it's not a popular name.
VARIATIONS: Narcessa, Narcisah, Nargis, Narissa, Nergis
FAMOUS NARCISSAS: Narcissa Malfoy is a character in the popular Harry Potter series of books and movies.

Nemo MEANING: nobody

{ *We couldn't care less about finding Nemo.* }

GENDER: male | **ORIGIN:** Latin | **RANKING:** not in the top 1,000
ETYMOLOGY: *Nemo* is Latin for nobody, so you might as well just name your child Loser or Who Needs You.
VARIATIONS: Nemoe, Nemow, Nemowe
FAMOUS NEMOS: Nemo is the name of a Pixar fish. It's also the name of the captain of the submarine *Nautilus*, found in Jules Verne's *Twenty Thousand Leagues under the Sea*.

Nerea MEANING: mine

{It's not always about you, Nerea. Geez.}

GENDER: female | **ORIGIN:** Basque | **RANKING:** 21 in Spain; not in the top 1,000 in the United States

ETYMOLOGY: Children are inherently selfish; it's their job. But to name a child Nerea, you must be a glutton for punishment. Nerea is from *nere*, which is Basque for mine. The Basque people live in a region that straddles Spain and France. Apparently, they love children whose first word isn't mama or dada but MINE MINE MINE!

VARIATIONS: Nereah, Neria, Neriah, Nyarea, Nyaria

Nevaeh MEANING: heaven spelled backwards

{Rehtie ti ecnuonorp ot woh wonk t'nod I. Oops . . . I mean: I don't know how to pronounce it either.}

GENDER: female | **ORIGIN:** American | **RANKING:** 35

ETYMOLOGY: In 2000, Sonny Sandoval, singer for Christian metal group P.O.D., named his daughter Nevaeh, which has many pronunciations. After that, the rare name became popular. A female wrestler who adopted the name may also have helped increase Nevaeh's popularity. Thus, the name has become popular due to its association with mindless popular culture. Heaven's sweet and all, but backwards and unpronounceable?

VARIATIONS: There are names that sound similar, but only Nevaeh is heaven spelled backwards.

The Pitter Patter of Little Proletariats

Acronymic names are not very common in the United States, but in the former Soviet Union, Bolsheviks and Bolshevikettes developed a mania for naming their children after the October Revolution (the revolution that led to the formation of the Soviet Union) and its leaders. The website Soviet-Empire.com offers many examples:

- Arvil (Armija V. I. Lenina): V. I. Lenin's Army
- Vektor (Velikij Kommunizm Torzhestvuet): Great Communism Triumphs
- Velior (Velikija Oktjabr'skaja Revoljucija): Great October Revolution
- Vidlen (Velikie Idei Lenina): Great Ideas of Lenin
- Vilen (V. I. Lenin): V. I. Lenin
- Donjera (Doch' Novoj Jery): Daughter of a New Era
- Krarmija (Krasnaja Armija): The Red Army
- Lestak (Lenin Stalin Kommunizm): Lenin Stalin Communism
- Lenora (Lenin Nashe Oruzhie): Lenin Is Our Weapon
- Revmark (Revoljucionnyj Marksizm): Revolutionary Marxism
- And one name summed it all up. Lorijerik (Lenin Oktjabr'skaja Revoljucija Industrializacija Jelektrifikacija Radiofikacija I Kommunizm): Lenin October Revolution Industrialization Electrification Radiofication and Communism

Noah MEANING: rest

{ Uh oh, little Noah's flooded his diaper again! }

GENDER: male | **ORIGIN:** Hebrew | **RANKING:** 5
ETYMOLOGY: *Noach*, from which Noah derives, means rest. The name might be a nice reminder of what parents used to get before they had children, a mortgage, a real job, and all those other bothersome adult responsibilities.
VARIATIONS: Noa, Noach, Noak, Noel, Noe

Nola MEANING: fair shoulder

{ She may have nice shoulders, but everything else, unfortunately, is butt ugly. }

GENDER: female | **ORIGIN:** Irish | **RANKING:** 888
ETYMOLOGY: Nola is a shortened form of the nearly impossible to spell Irish-rooted name Fionnuala, which is related to the words "fair shoulder." If you have to emphasize the beauty of the shoulder, then the rest of her must be pretty unpleasant. However, the name might have a different etymology altogether. A popular name in the nineteenth century, Nola had all but disappeared by the middle of the twentieth. Then, in 2005, it began to reappear. Hurricane Katrina nearly wiped out New Orleans that year, and NOLA is a popular acronym for New Orleans.
VARIATIONS: Finola, Nilla, Fenella

Obama MEANING: slightly bent

{ Hail to the slightly bent chief! }

GENDER: male | **ORIGIN:** Kenyan | **RANKING:** Obama is not in the top 1,000 and neither, for that matter, is Barack. Nonetheless, newspaper stories from 2008 reported an increasing number of parents choosing one of these names for their future (crooked) presidents-to-be.

ETYMOLOGY: Now it can be told! President Barack Obama is crooked! Well, at least his name is. *Obama* is Kenyan for slightly bent. Shhh. Don't tell Rush Limbaugh.

VARIATIONS: Obeoma, Obioma, Obamah, Obyoma, Obyomah

Odessa **MEANING:** to hate

{When Odessa says she hates her sister, watch out!}

GENDER: female | **ORIGIN:** Greek | **RANKING:** not in the top 1,000

ETYMOLOGY: Odessa is from the Greek *odyssami*, which means to hate. Such a nice name for a pretty little girl.

VARIATIONS: Odesa, Oddessa, Oddesa

FAMOUS ODESSAS: Odessa is one of the largest cities in Ukraine. It contains the Potemkin Stairs, site of a famous scene in director Sergei Eisenstein's *The Battleship Potemkin*.

Ola **MEANING:** ancestor's relic

{She's like something you'd find sitting around in your attic.}

GENDER: unisex | **ORIGIN:** Norse | **RANKING:** not in the top 1,000

ETYMOLOGY: *Ola* is Old Norse for ancestor's relic or ancestor's relative. What's that musty smell? Oh, it's just Ola! It's time to change her mothballs again.

VARIATIONS: Olah, Olla, Ollah

FAMOUS OLAS: Ola Ray is the model and actress who played Michael Jackson's girlfriend in the famous, feature-length video for Jackson's song "Thriller."

Olivia MEANING: elf army

{*Pick up your little bitty swords and follow me!
Charge!*}

GÉNDER: female | **ORIGIN:** German | **RANKING:** 4
ETYMOLOGY: Olivia is the feminine form of Oliver. Oliver is based on the
Germanic name Alfher. Alfher is made up of the words *alf* (elf) and *hari*
(army). We tend to think of elves as benign creatures, but they must have
been some fierce little buggers once upon a time. And if Olivia is of short
stature, then her friends and colleagues will drown her in elf jokes.
VARIATIONS: Alivya, Alivia, Olivie, Oliwia, Livia

Oscar MEANING: deer lover

{*Dude, we have got to get you a woman.*}

GENDER: male | **ORIGIN:** Irish | **RANKING:** 162
ETYMOLOGY: Oscar derives from the Gaelic *os* (deer) and *cara* (lover).
Oh dear!
VARIATIONS: Oscarito, Oskar, Osgar, Osku, Oszkar
FAMOUS OSCARS: Irish author Oscar Wilde got in trouble for allegedly
engaging in an improper sexual relationship . . . though not with a deer.
Oscar the Grouch is the crankiest resident of Sesame Street.

Ovid MEANING: sheep

{*We chose the name because we wanted him to
be easily led.*}

GENDER: male | **ORIGIN:** Latin | **RANKING:** not in the top 1,000
ETYMOLOGY: Ovid comes from *ovis*, Latin for sheep. If you're looking
for a follower, just look for Ovid. He'll go anywhere you tell him to.
VARIATIONS: Ofid, Ofidd, Ofyd, Oved, Ovydio
FAMOUS OVIDS: Poetry comes naturally to Ovids. Ovid was a first-
century Roman poet, and Ovid Densusiano (1873–1938) was a
Romanian poet who brought modernism to Romanian literature.

Stupid Sports Names: Just Plain Stupid Edition

Cheering on the Bills or the Bears or the Chargers is easy. Those teams sound strong and powerful. But cheering on the Banana Slugs? Some team names are just . . . well, stupid.

- If it had been left solely to university officials, the University of California, Santa Cruz's athletics mascot would be a sea lion. Students and athletes rejected that name, opting instead for banana slugs. Why? Well, keep in mind that this is the branch of U.C. that has a substantial Grateful Dead archive.

- Quick! Give me a professional sports team named for a mark of punctuation. At least one exists: The Winston-Salem (North Carolina) Dash. The Chicago White Sox farm team decided to name itself after the dash in Winston-Salem in time for the 2009 season. "Dash" makes sense because players dash from base to base. What makes this stupid? That mark of punctuation between Winston and Salem is a *hyphen*!

- The Dash isn't the only stupidly named team in Winston-Salem. Wake Forest University has the Demon Deacons. Deacons are church officials (Wake Forest was founded by the North Carolina Baptist State Convention). Demons are Satan's minions. Put the two together and you get . . . what exactly?

Paige   MEANING: servant

{She just started walking, and already her parents have trained her to bring them their coffee!}

GENDER: female (though occasionally used for males) | **ORIGIN:** Greek, English | **RANKING:** 107

ETYMOLOGY: Paige began as the Greek *paidon*, meaning little boy, because most servants used to be little boys. Over time, that word developed into page, which still means errand boy or errand girl. The name returns the *i* to the word. You could just name the girl Gofer (go fer coffee, go fer lunch orders) and save yourself the trouble.

VARIATIONS: Page, Paege, Paese, Paise, Payge

Pamela   MEANING: all sweetness

{Just saying your name makes my teeth ache.}

GENDER: female | **ORIGIN:** coined by poet Sir Philip Sidney | **RANKING:** 967

ETYMOLOGY: Pamela is a common name that was coined by a writer. Sir Philip Sidney created the name in the late sixteenth century. He used the Greek elements *pan* (all) and *meli* (honey; sweetness). Now all of this may sound well and good, but someone named Pamela is going to be as sickeningly sweet as Pollyanna, a name which may have been coined by children's author Eleanor H. Porter.

VARIATIONS: Pamalla, Pamelah, Pameleigh, Pamelie, Pammelie

Parker
MEANING: park keeper

{I don't mind picking up the empty cans so much, but the used condoms . . .}

GENDER: male | **ORIGIN:** English | **RANKING:** 79

ETYMOLOGY: Parker began as an English surname for people who took care of parks, which sounds like a better job than it is . . . unless you like wearing fluorescent vests and picking up trash with a stick.

VARIATIONS: Parkar, Parke, Parkes, Parkman, Parks

FAMOUS PARKERS: Actress Parker Posey was in so many indie films during the 1990s that she earned the sobriquet "Queen of the Indies." Charlie Parker revolutionized jazz as one of the founders of bebop.

Paul
MEANING: small

{Oh, you are standing up.}

GENDER: male | **ORIGIN:** Latin | **RANKING:** 187

ETYMOLOGY: From the Latin *paulus*, Paul means small or humble. The name has been popular since Saint Paul helped bring Christ's message to the masses. In our super-sized society, most people look down their noses at anything small . . . despite that silly old saw that good things come in small packages.

VARIATIONS: Paley, Paol, Pavlov, Pollard, Powell

Penelope
MEANING: weft over her face

{We're naming the next one Bag Over Her Face.}

GENDER: female | **ORIGIN:** Greek | **RANKING:** 169

ETYMOLOGY: Penelope derives from *pene* (weft) and *ops* (face). This is the Greek version of putting a bag over her head.

VARIATIONS: Pelcha, Penelopee, Peni, Penina, Nellie

Persephone MEANING: bringer of death

{ *We should have just named her Black Widow.* }

GENDER: female | **ORIGIN:** Greek | **RANKING:** not in the top 1,000
ETYMOLOGY: Persephone comes from the Greek words *pherein pho-non*, or bringer of death. Persephone was one of Zeus's illegitimate daughters and became queen of the underworld. Persephone carries out the curses men make on the souls of the dead who reside in her kingdom. Dang, Persephone is one scary queen of the underworld.
VARIATIONS: Peri, Persefone, Persefonee, Persefonie, Seffi
FAMOUS PERSEPHONES: Since Persephone was the wife of Pluto, Persephone is one name science-fiction writers such as Douglas Adams's (*The Hitchhiker's Guide to the Galaxy*) have ascribed to made-up planets beyond Pluto . . . when Pluto was still a planet, that is.

Peter MEANING: rock

{ *He's like a rock . . . only dumber.* }

GENDER: male | **ORIGIN:** Latin | **RANKING:** 198
ETYMOLOGY: Peter is from the Latin *petrus*, or rock. Rocks symbolize strength, but they also suggest stubbornness. In addition, rocks are what can be found in the heads of stupid people . . . and in the hands of playground bullies.
VARIATIONS: Patch, Pearce, Pedro, Pierre, Piers
FAMOUS PETERS: Ironically, the apostle of Christ whom Jesus chris-tened Peter was anything but decisive and rock steady. Immediately after Christ's capture, Peter denied three times that he even knew the guy.

Philip MEANING: lover of horses

{ *It's okay to love horses; it's just not okay to love horses.* }

GENDER: male | **ORIGIN:** Greek | **RANKING:** 406

ETYMOLOGY: Philip derives from the Greek words *philein* (love) and *hippos* (horse). Thus, if you want to name your child after one of Christ's apostles, choose a name like John, which means God is merciful. Philip suggests bestiality, you freak.

VARIATIONS: Phillip, Felipe, Phelps, Flip, Pip

Phineas   MEANING: snake's mouth

{How much uglier than a serpent's tooth is Phineas?}

GENDER: male | **ORIGIN:** Hebrew | **RANKING:** not in the top 1,000

ETYMOLOGY: Phineas derives from the Hebrew *peh* (mouth) and *nahash* (snake). Snakes are slimy. Snakes' mouths contain fangs that drip venom and forked tongues. If you speak with a forked tongue, then you're a liar. Snakes probably have bad breath. Gross name . . . any way you look at it.

VARIATIONS: Finny, Phinehas, Phinneas, Phinny, Pinchus

FAMOUS PHINEASES: Phineas Flynn is the triangular-headed half of the Disney Channel's popular cartoon *Phineas and Ferb*.

Phyllis   MEANING: foliage

{Damn, I sliced my ball into Phyllis.}

GENDER: female | **ORIGIN:** Greek | **RANKING:** not in the top 1,000

ETYMOLOGY: Phyllis is from a Greek word, spelled the same way, which means foliage, tree, branch, or leaf. Basically, anyone named Phyllis is named after a generic clump of bushes. In addition, the name originates in a tragic story from Greek mythology where Phyllis hanged herself for love. The gods took pity on her and turned her into a tree. Does any parent want their child to die for love and be turned into a tree? Didn't think so.

VARIATIONS: Fillis, Philis, Phylicia, Phylyss, Filide

FAMOUS PHYLLISES: Phyllis Diller (1917–2012) began her stand-up comedy career in 1955. Phyllis Smith plays Phyllis Lapin-Vance on *The Office*.

Windy Wild Garlic

Chicago's name stinks. Literally. The Windy City is synonymous with many things: deep-dish pizza, crooked politicians, and the losingest team in Major League Baseball (the Cubs, of course), among others. But you'd better hope the wind isn't blowing in your direction, because the city's name derives from *shikaakwa*, a word in the Miami-Illinois language that meant wild garlic or wild onion. The French, who "discovered" *shikaakwa*, shifted the name ultimately to Chicago. Chicago isn't the only town in the world with a terrible name, though.

- Kabul, the capital of Afghanistan, means crooked or hunch-backed.
- Lalibela, Ethiopia, is known for its churches, many of which are carved out of rock. At one time, however, it must have been known for people who flap their gums too much. Its name means person who talks too much.
- And Accra, the capital of Ghana, means ants. People probably don't picnic there much.

Porsche MEANING: pig

{Mmmm. Bacon.}

GENDER: female | **ORIGIN:** Latin | **RANKING:** not in the top 1,000
ETYMOLOGY: So, you thought you'd give your little girl a classy name? You figured naming her after a luxury car would be the perfect choice. Well the joke's on you, parvenu. Porsche is the feminine form of *porcius*, or pig. Just name her Porky and be done with it.
VARIATIONS: Portia, Porshay, Porshe, Perse
FAMOUS PORSCHES: In addition to the car make that bears his name, Ferdinand Porsche (1875–1951) also invented the iconic Volkswagen Beetle.

Porter MEANING: porter

{We didn't want children. We wanted slaves.}

GENDER: unisex | **ORIGIN:** Latin, English | **RANKING:** 450
ETYMOLOGY: Porter began with the Latin word for door, *porta*, and became a last name derived from the occupation of opening doors and carrying suitcases. There's nothing wrong with opening doors and carrying suitcases for a living, but don't you want your next generation to aspire to some form of skilled labor?
VARIATIONS: Portar, Portyr, Portier, Pryderi, Proterio

Priscilla MEANING: old, ancient

{She didn't get pimples. She got liver spots.}

GENDER: female | **ORIGIN:** Latin | **RANKING:** 487
ETYMOLOGY: Prim, proper, prissy Priscilla. The name originates with *priscus*, Latin for old or ancient. As soon as she's potty trained, you can buy Prissy her first pair of granny panties. Adorable!
VARIATIONS: Percilla, Presilla, Priss, Cilla, Prissy

Q & R

Quella MEANING: kill

{ *I've got one piece of advice for you: Don't make Quella mad.* }

GENDER: female | **ORIGIN:** English | **RANKING:** not in the top 1,000
ETYMOLOGY: Quella derives from the Old English *cweald*, which means kill. Could that be why this name isn't very popular?
VARIATIONS: Laquela, Quela, Quelia, Quellah, Quiana

Quigley MEANING: one with messy hair

{ *Maybe you've never seen this, Quigley. It's called* hair spray, *and you can borrow mine.* }

GENDER: male | **ORIGIN:** Irish | **RANKING:** not in the top 1,000
ETYMOLOGY: Quigley derives from a Gaelic surname, the meaning of which was something like one with messy hair. Better put a comb on that baby registry.
VARIATIONS: Quiggley, Quiggly, Quiglea, Quiglee, Quig
FAMOUS QUIGLEYS: Joan Quigley is the astrologer famous for prognosticating President Ronald Reagan's future.

Your Daily Name

The name of American actress Tuesday Weld notwithstanding, days of the week don't typically make for popular names. Besides, Weld's birth name was Susan, so she doesn't even count. And while you might find the occasional Sunday or Wednesday, they're not commonly used for names. Different languages/countries, however, are another matter. Some African countries, for example, have a tendency to choose names related to the day on which a child is born.

- Names meaning Monday: Adjoa (Ghana, female), Kodjo (Ghana, male), Senen (Indonesia, male)
- Names meaning Tuesday: Kwabena (Ghana, male), Mardi (French, female)
- Names meaning Wednesday: Abeeku (Ghana, male)
- Names meaning Thursday: Castiel (angel of Thursday, Latin, unisex), Lakia (Sanskrit, female)
- Names meaning Friday: Afia (Ghana, female), Kofi (Ghana, male)
- Names meaning Saturday: Kwame (Ghana, male)
- Names meaning Sunday: Akosua (Ghana, female), Kwasi (Ghana, male), Nedelya (Bulgaria, female), Nomasonto (Nguni, female), Sabiti (Uganada, male)

Quimby MEANING: woman's house

{ *Yeah, I've been in your* **mama's** *house.* }

GENDER: male | **ORIGIN:** Scandinavian | **RANKING:** not in the top 1,000

ETYMOLOGY: Quimby is a guy's name that derives from the Scandinavian words meaning woman's house. A masculine name for a masculine guy!

VARIATIONS: Quembee, Quembey, Quemby, Quenby, Quinby

FAMOUS QUIMBYS: Darius Quimby was the first law enforcement officer killed in the line of duty in the United States. He was shot by Whiting Sweeting on January 3, 1791, while trying to serve a trespassing warrant. Sweeting was caught and hanged a few months later.

Quincy MEANING: fifth

{ *You're first in our family, but fifth in our hearts!* }

GENDER: male | **ORIGIN:** Latin | **RANKING:** 599

ETYMOLOGY: Quincy comes from the Roman given name Quintus, meaning fifth. As if coming in fourth place wasn't bad enough . . .

VARIATIONS: Quenci, Quince, Quincee, Quinci, Quinn

FAMOUS QUINCYS: Composer/producer Quincy Jones may be best known as the producer of Michael Jackson's immortal *Thriller* album (1982).

Rachel MEANING: ewe (female sheep)

{ *Now be a good little girl and drink the Kool-Aid.* }

GENDER: female | **ORIGIN:** Hebrew | **RANKING:** 117

ETYMOLOGY: From the Hebrew word *rahel*, meaning ewe, the biblical Rachel was Jacob's wife and the mother of Joseph (he of the amazing Technicolor dreamcoat). Most Rachels would not want anyone to know that they were named for farm animals that poop copiously.

VARIATIONS: Rachael, Racheal, Raquel, Raychel, Raychelle

Rain

MEANING: water that falls from the sky and ruins most outdoor activities

{ *Rain, Rain, go away. Don't come again another day.* }

GENDER: unisex | **ORIGIN:** Hippy | **RANKING:** not in the top 1,000
ETYMOLOGY: For some, Rain may simply be a nickname for Lorraine, which comes from Lorraine in France. For others, Rain, Rainn, and Raine derive most likely from parents who grew up in the 1960s, smoked quite a bit of dope, and found the Grateful Dead a sublime— rather than an intensely boring—experience.
VARIATIONS: Raine, Rainn, Rainer
FAMOUS RAINS: Actor Rainn Wilson plays Dwight Schrute on *The Office*. Much like unwanted precipitation, Dwight is a nuisance to everyone.

Rakeem

MEANING: based on a member of the Wu-Tang Clan

{ *He really is a natural-born gangsta.* }

GENDER: male | **ORIGIN:** RZA | **RANKING:** not in the top 1,000
ETYMOLOGY: The exact origins of this name are unclear, but Rakeem began to become a popular name, especially among African-American families, in 1992. In 1991, Robert Fitzgerald Diggs released a popular hip-hop EP, *Ooh I Love You Rakeem*. A few years later, Diggs became RZA and a founding member of hardcore rap supergroup the Wu-Tang Clan.
VARIATIONS: Raheem, Rakeme, Rakeim
FAMOUS RAKEEMS: Rakeem Christmas is a power forward for the University of Syracuse's basketball team who has generated a lot of NBA scouting buzz.

Ramsey

MEANING: wild garlic island

{ *Dude, try a breath mint!* }

GENDER: male | **ORIGIN:** English | **RANKING:** not in the top 1,000

ETYMOLOGY: Ramsey began as an English surname, designating some-one from the "wild garlic island." Where is the wild garlic island? That's been lost to history, but the men there probably didn't have to worry about vampires (garlic repels them) or dating women (garlic repels them). A cute nickname for Ramsey might be Stink Breath.

VARIATIONS: Ramsay, Ramsea, Ramsee, Ramsie, Ramzea, Ramzy

FAMOUS RAMSEYS: Ramsey Clark is a progressive activist who served as President Lyndon Johnson's attorney general from 1967 to 1969. More recently, he served on the legal defense teams of such contro-versial figures as Saddam Hussein and former Serbian president (and alleged perpetrator of genocide) Slobodan Milosevic.

Rebecca   MEANING: to tie, to bind

{*Fifty Shades of Grey's got nothing on her!*}

GENDER: female | **ORIGIN:** Hebrew | **RANKING:** 148

ETYMOLOGY: Rebecca derives from the Hebrew *ribqa*, which means to tie or to bind. The Bible suggests that the name doesn't refer to bond-age or serial killers, but to the bonds of marriage. Some men, of course, would rather be taken away by a serial killer than tied down by mar-riage to Rebecca or anyone else. Besides, Rebecca was dishonest and played favorites. She was married to Isaac and helped Jacob (one of her sons with Isaac) steal his brother Esau's birthright.

VARIATIONS: Bekka, Rebakah, Becky, Rebekkah, Rabecca

Reese   MEANING: rashness

{*Hey y'all, watch this! I'm gonna set off this cherry bomb in my back pocket!*}

GENDER: unisex, typically female | **ORIGIN:** Welsh | **RANKING:** 130

ETYMOLOGY: Reese is the feminine form of Rhys, a Welsh name/word that means enthusiasm, ardor, or rashness. A career in law enforcement is not recommended for someone named Reese. She's the type who will shoot first and ask questions later.

VARIATIONS: Reace, Rease, Reise, Rhett, Ryse

FAMOUS REESES: The name became popular for girls thanks in part to actress Reese Witherspoon, who earned an Academy Award for her performance as June Carter Cash in the Johnny Cash biopic, *Walk the Line*.

Remy   MEANING: oarsman

{Stroke! Stroke! Stroke!}

GENDER: unisex | **ORIGIN:** Latin | **RANKING:** 881

ETYMOLOGY: Remy stems from *remigis*, the Latin word for oarsman. Perhaps one day he will be the captain of his Ivy League sculling team. Or he will steer the ship of state. Or, more likely, he'll just be some tiny cog in some big industry wheel, endlessly rowing to nowhere.

VARIATIONS: Remi, Rahim (male), Remee, Remi, Remmey

Reuben   MEANING: behold, a son

{How did I get the nickname Drop Trou? Well, you see . . .}

GENDER: male | **ORIGIN:** Hebrew | **RANKING:** 942

ETYMOLOGY: *Reuben* means "behold, a son" in Hebrew. The biblical Reuben was Jacob's firstborn son. There might have been a little penis envy going around the village when Reuben made his first appearance at show and tell.

VARIATIONS: Ruben, Reubin, Rheuben, Rhuben, Rouvin

FAMOUS REUBENS: Reuben "Rube" Goldberg (1883–1970) was a cartoonist who depicted complex machines that performed simple tasks. Think of the game Mouse Trap that you may have played as a kid.

Henry the Beautiful

Columbus sailed the ocean blue in 1492, yet he got shafted when it came to the name of the land he "discovered." Why did Italian explorer Amerigo Vespucci (1454–1512), rather than Columbus, get naming rights for the Americas? Because he figured out something Columbus never accepted. Columbus believed his discovery was the outskirts of Asia, whereas Vespucci figured out the new landmass was one previously unknown to explorers. As a result, German cartographer Martin Waldseemüller (1470–1520) labeled the new land America. Americus is the Latinized version of Vespucci's first name, which Waldseemüller made feminine—America. But wait, as the TV pitchmen say, there's more. Amerigo is an Italian form of a medieval Latin name, Emericus, which is an early form of the common name Henry. That's right. We're in the United States of Henry.

Rhett   MEANING: speaker

{*Frankly, my dear, I wish you'd shut the hell up.*}

GENDER: unisex | **ORIGIN:** Dutch | **RANKING:** 563

ETYMOLOGY: Rhett is the Anglicized version of the Dutch surname, de Raedt. *Raedt* means advice or counsel. The name suggests someone who never listens and won't stop talking. In other words, a typical guy.

VARIATIONS: Ret, Rett, Rhet, Rhette

FAMOUS RHETTS: Long after her death, Margaret Mitchell still makes ladies' hearts flutter over Rhett Butler, the hero/cad of her 1936 novel, *Gone with the Wind.*

Rhona   MEANING: rough island

{*Girl, you're looking rough! Guess you can't help it.*}

GENDER: female | **ORIGIN:** Scottish | **RANKING:** not in the top 1,000

ETYMOLOGY: Rhona stems from a Scottish island, Rona, which means "rough island." Very far north, the rocky, cold island must have been (and still is) pretty inhospitable. Rhona will be the kind of girl who looks like she's always recovering from a hangover: bedhead, red eyes, disheveled clothes, etc.

VARIATIONS: Rona, Rowena, Rhoni, Ronna

FAMOUS RHONAS: Rhona Bennett was a member of R&B group En Vogue from 2003 to 2008. She also is known for her recurring role as Nicole on *The Jamie Foxx Show.*

Rhonda   MEANING: noisy

{*Help me, Rhonda, and shut up already!*}

GENDER: female | **ORIGIN:** Welsh | **RANKING:** not in the top 1,000

ETYMOLOGY: Rhonda comes from the Rhondda (noisy) Valley in Wales, which was coal mined into oblivion. In its heyday, the sounds of the

Industrial Revolution in action must have been deafening. Enjoy life with your adorable little loud mouth.

VARIATIONS: Rhona, Rondah, Rhondea, Ronelle, Ronette

FAMOUS RHONDAS: Missouri-born Rhonda Vincent is a bluegrass artist who plays multiple instruments and sings. The *Wall Street Journal* named her "the new Queen of Bluegrass."

Rin   MEANING: cold hearted

{*Little Rin can just spend hours outside sizzling ants with her magnifying glass!*}

GENDER: unisex, typically female | **ORIGIN:** Japanese |
RANKING: 6 in Japan; not in the top 1,000 in the United States
ETYMOLOGY: In addition to naming your child after a heroic, fictional dog (Rin Tin Tin), *rin* is a Japanese word that means severe or cold . . . as in cold-hearted. Don't count on Rin to take care of you in your old age. She'll just give you a poorly written, handmade sign and send you to the nearest interstate off-ramp.

VARIATIONS: Rinako, Rini, Ryn, Rynn

Ripley   MEANING: cleared strip of land

{*My nickname is Clearcut.*}

GENDER: unisex, typically male | **ORIGIN:** English |
RANKING: not in the top 1,000
ETYMOLOGY: Ripley began as an English surname, borrowed from a place designation. In other words, the Ripleys were from a place that had been clearcut. Someone named Ripley is not likely to have much of a future in the Environmental Protection Agency, or in Democratic politics.

VARIATIONS: Riplea, Riplee, Ripply, Rypley, Rip

FAMOUS RIPLEYS: One famous *female* Ripley is Sigourney Weaver's character in the *Alien* film series. She mowed down aliens, much like lumber companies mow down forests. As a last name, the most famous Ripley is Robert L. Ripley, who created *Ripley's Believe It or Not!* in 1919.

Moxie Crimefighter and Kal-El to the Rescue!

Three words: celebrity baby names. Three letters: WTF!

- Comedian/magician Penn Jillette and his wife Emily named their child Moxie Crimefighter Jillette.
- Not to be outdone in the crime fighter department, Nicolas Cage and Alice Kim named their child Kal-El Coppola Cage. Kal-El is Superman's Kryptonian birth name.
- Real-life do-gooder Bob Geldof, whose Live Aid brought attention to the plight of world hunger, seems to love humanity. But his children . . . not so much. He and Paula Yates named their children Fifi-Trixibelle, Little Pixie, and Peaches Honeyblossom. Maybe it's not Sir Bob's fault, though. Paula Yates named her daughter with INXS singer Michael Hutchence Heavenly Hiraani Tiger Lily Hutchence.
- And finally, Bono, who wants to save everything and everyone, named his child—with wife Alison—Elijah Bob Patricus Guggi Q Hewson. Bono's real name is Paul Hewson.

Rocco MEANING: rest

{ *Sure he's lazy, but he's all we've got.* }

GENDER: male | **ORIGIN:** German | **RANKING:** 402
ETYMOLOGY: Rocco derives from *hroc*, a German word meaning rest. Despite its Germanic origins, the name is typically associated with people of Italian descent: Tampa Bay Rays coach Rocco Baldelli, boxer Rocco "Rocky" Marciano, celebrity chef Rocco DiSpirito, and the list goes on and on. Possibly, the Italian Rocco comes from the Italian *rocca*, which means fortress. So Rocco will either be a gigantic, ball-busting bad ass or a terminally lazy ne'er-do-well.
VARIATIONS: Rocca, Roche, Rockea, Rocki, Rockey

Rochelle MEANING: roar, battle cry

{ *This is Rochelle, and this is her sister, Rebel Yell.* }

GENDER: female | **ORIGIN:** German | **RANKING:** not in the top 1,000
ETYMOLOGY: From the German *rohon*, meaning battle cry or roar, Rochelle will be the terror of the playground, captain of the cheerleading squad, and finally, a talking head on one of those new programs where the hosts won't allow their guests to finish a complete sentence.
VARIATIONS: Rashelle, Richelle, Rochella, Rochette, Rushelle
FAMOUS ROCHELLES: Rochelle Alers is a romance novelist with two million books in print. Rochelle Ballard is a professional surfer.

Rocky MEANING: rocky

{ *And the winner of this year's Nobel Prize in Physics is . . . Rocky? Nah.* }

GENDER: male | **ORIGIN:** English | **RANKING:** not in the top 1,000
ETYMOLOGY: Rocky began to become popular in the middle of the twentieth century due to boxer Rocky Marciano, one of the most successful fighters in the history of the sport. Marciano's real first name

was Rocco (see earlier entry), but parents glommed onto his nickname. The name peaked again in the 1970s thanks to Sylvester Stallone's *Rocky*, a great film followed by a plethora of sucky sequels. Thus, Rocky definitely suggests tough, but it also evokes someone with rocks in his head screaming, "Adrian!"

VARIATIONS: Roc, Rocco, Rockey, Rocki, Roque

FAMOUS ROCKYS: African percussionist Rocky Dzidzornu added conga sizzle to the Rolling Stones's "Sympathy for the Devil."

Ronan MEANING: little seal

{*Little Ronan's already bouncing a ball on his nose!*}

GENDER: male | **ORIGIN:** Irish | **RANKING:** 458

ETYMOLOGY: The Gaelic word *ron* and the diminutive *an* form the words little seal. If he can't make it into college, then at least Ronan can run away and join the circus.

VARIATIONS: Ronann, Ronen, Ronin, Ronnan, Ronyn

Rosamund MEANING: horse protection

{*I've gotta see a girl about a horse.*}

GENDER: female | **ORIGIN:** German, Latin | **RANKING:** not in the top 1,000

ETYMOLOGY: The problem with this name is that it doesn't mean what some parents think it means. They believe it's from the Latin phrase *rosa mundi*, which means rose of the world. That's a delightful name for a young lady. However, Rosamund originates with the German words *hros* (horse) and *mund* (protection). Horse protection? Um, not so pretty.

VARIATIONS: Rosamunda, Rosamunde, Rakhshonda, Rosenda, Rosinda

FAMOUS ROSAMUNDS: Rosamund Clifford (1150–1176) was a mistress of England's King Henry II. Her beauty is legendary, and she was known as Rose of the World. This is the Rosamund who helped change the true meaning of Rosamund to the prettier meaning, "pure rose."

Stupid Band Names

Not every band can be named The Beatles. Their name was a clever way to evoke beat music while giving a nod to Buddy Holly's band, The Crickets. But, for every clever band name, there are countless stupid ones.

- Perry Farrell's first band, Jane's Addiction, played on both drug addiction and "addiction" to a favorite band. His next group was called Porno for Pyros. He thought of the name while watching the L.A. riots of the early 1990s. Yes, it's alliterative. But as Cracked.com points out, how, exactly, is pornography for pyromaniacs any different from regular pornography?
- Def Leppard was among the better hair-metal bands of the 1980s. Singer Joe Elliott came up with the name Deaf Leopard while in school. He thought it was cool, apparently. The misspelled version of the final name gives a nod to the equally-spelling-challenged Led Zeppelin, and leopards are sleek and vicious. But deaf? Isn't that just asking people to say that your music is so unlistenable that even the creature in your band's name doesn't want to hear it?

Sabra   MEANING: thorny cactus

{Stop being such a prick!}

GENDER: female | **ORIGIN:** Hebrew | **RANKING:** not in the top 1,000

ETYMOLOGY: Sabra could simply be a diminutive of Sabrina, but *sabra* is also Hebrew slang for a thorny cactus with a sweet interior. It may be sweet on the inside, but it will scar you up if you get too close to it.

VARIATIONS: Sabara, Sabarah, Sabarra, Sabira, Sabraa

FAMOUS SABRAS: Sabra Johnson was the champion on the third season of Fox's *So You Think You Can Dance*.

Sawyer   MEANING: one who saws wood

{He's a lumberjack, and he's okay.}

GENDER: male | **ORIGIN:** English | **RANKING:** 172

ETYMOLOGY: Sawyer began as a last name for people who saw wood, a phrase that has since been used to describe snoring. Thus, anyone named Sawyer will most likely be boring. If you're boring parents, then that's fine. Give boring parties. Watch boring home movies. Have boring children. Whatever.

VARIATIONS: Saer, Sawer, Sawier, Sawyers, Sayre

Selah MEANING: stop

{Selah! In the name of love!}

GENDER: female | **ORIGIN:** Hebrew | **RANKING:** 579

ETYMOLOGY: *Selah* is a word found often in the Book of Psalms, and it doesn't have an exact translation. Basically, it's a command that the reader should stop and think about what he or she has just read. It's a constant interrupter that can be pretty annoying. Thus, Selah will constantly interrupt you with stupid questions, which really just makes her a typical child, doesn't it?

VARIATIONS: Sela, Saheala, Saheela, Sahela, Sahelee

Selena MEANING: moon

{Girl, what is your deal with always sticking your butt in people's faces?}

GENDER: female | **ORIGIN:** Greek, Spanish | **RANKING:** 321

ETYMOLOGY: The name Selena (a Spanish name) began as Selene, a Greek goddess of the moon. Her Roman equivalent is the better-known Luna. Full moons cause lunacy . . . such as the idea that mooning someone is cool.

VARIATIONS: Saleana, Selene, Saleanah, Silenia, Celenia

FAMOUS SELENAS: Selena is a Spanish name that was only mildly popular until the emergence and tragic death of singer Selena Quintanilla-Pérez (1971–1995), known simply as Selena. The year of her death, the name rose all the way to ranking 95. As a name, Selena has dropped off since, but it has begun a slow rise since actress-singer Selena Gomez arrived on the scene.

Semaj   MEANING: James spelled backwards

{Welcome to the Backward Names Club.
Semaj, meet Nevaeh. Nevaeh, meet Semaj.}

GENDER: male | **ORIGIN:** James | **RANKING:** 630

ETYMOLOGY: In the waning years of the twentieth century, a pioneer whose name is lost to history devised the brilliant plan to name his or her child James spelled backwards. Since then, this essentially meaningless name has continued to rise in popularity. Semaj, by the way, also happens to be Australian slang for the f-word.

VARIATIONS: It's not exactly a real name, so there are no variations.

Seneca   MEANING: old, place of stones

{You're not only old; you've got rocks in your
head!}

GENDER: male | **ORIGIN:** Latin, Native American | **RANKING:** not in the top 1,000

ETYMOLOGY: Confusion and apple juice doom this name. Seneca could be from the Latin *senectus*, which means old. That's rotten. Seneca is also the name of a Native American tribe that once flourished in New York before being decimated by European immigrants. That's not auspicious. In addition, the Seneca nation's chosen name means People of the Great Hill, which is cool. However, since Seneca sounded like another tribe's word for People from the Place of Stones, most people think Seneca has to do with a bunch of rocks. And finally, Seneca is a popular brand name of apple juice, a beverage that's drunk only by children who are forced to imbibe it. Whatever way you slice it, having the name Seneca makes you a bad seed.

VARIATIONS: Senaka, Seneka, Samuka, Senecca, Senequa

Kelly Hildebrandt to Wed Kelly Hildebrandt

Boredom, Facebook, unisex names, and coincidence sometimes can be the ingredients for a successful relationship . . .

In April 2008, Florida twenty-something Kelly Hildebrandt was bored and logged on to the popular social-networking site, Facebook. She decided to put her name into the "search" space and found . . . a twenty-something Texas man with the same unusual name. Female Kelly wrote to male Kelly, just noting it was odd that they had the same name. Male Kelly found female Kelly's profile photo favorable, and the afar flirting began.

A few weeks later, male Kelly visited Florida. The two found that—in addition to sharing a name—they also share a love of the beach and cooking, among other things. Before long, male Kelly relocated to Florida and proposed to female Kelly in December. Ten months—and a thorough genealogical search to make sure they weren't somehow related—later, Kelly Hildebrandt and Kelly Hildebrandt got married. Let the future—and mass confusion—begin!

Sergio   MEANING: servant

{Sergio, go get coffee. Sergio, make these copies. Sergio, get a life.}

GENDER: male | **ORIGIN:** Roman, Etruscan | **RANKING:** 278
ETYMOLOGY: Sergio is a Spanish, Italian, and Portuguese version of the Roman or Etruscan name Sergius, which means servant. Thanks to designer jeans company Sergio Valente (which is not named for a real person, by the way), the name became chic. However, based on its actual meaning, anyone named Sergio will be condemned to the life of a servile sycophant.
VARIATIONS: Sergei, Sachairi, Saguaro, Sergi, Serge

Shae   MEANING: hawk-like

{She's so cute . . . until her talons come out.}

GENDER: female | **ORIGIN:** Irish | **RANKING:** not in the top 1,000
ETYMOLOGY: Shae is from the Gaelic *seaghdha*, meaning hawk-like. Hawks are beautiful and majestic. They have amazing eyesight. They scoop up cute, tiny, woodland creatures and smaller (probably cute) birds, kill them, and eat them. Oops. Well, two out of three ain't bad.
VARIATIONS: Shay, Shea, Lashay, Shaw, Seaghdh
FAMOUS SHAES: Actress Shae D'Lyn had a recurring role (Jane Cavanaugh) on the 1990s television sitcom *Dharma & Greg*. In addition, she has starred in such films as *Vegas Vacation*.

Shanna   MEANING: old, ancient

{She was born with crow's feet and worry lines.}

GENDER: female | **ORIGIN:** Irish | **RANKING:** not in the top 1,000
ETYMOLOGY: Shanna comes from the Gaelic *sean*, meaning old and ancient. Talk about an old soul!

VARIATIONS: Seanna, Shannon, Shawna, Shoshannah, Susanna

FAMOUS SHANNAS: Reality television star Shanna Moakler (*Bridalplasty*, *Meet the Barkers*) began her career as first runner-up in the 1995 Miss USA pageant. She's also well known for her, um, involved personal life.

Shannon   MEANING: old river

{She may be stagnant and smelly, but she's my wife!}

GENDER: unisex, typically female | **ORIGIN:** Irish | **RANKING:** 706

ETYMOLOGY: This name derives from the Shannon River, Ireland's longest. That river's name comes from the Gaelic *sean* (old) and *abhann* (river). Old rivers have had centuries to be polluted by animal and toxic waste. Yum!

VARIATIONS: Shana, Shanna, Shannah, Shannen, Shanon

Sharon   MEANING: plain

{We wanted a name that fell somewhere between fugly and hot.}

GENDER: female | **ORIGIN:** Hebrew | **RANKING:** 823

ETYMOLOGY: *Sharon* is Hebrew for plain, as in "fruited plain." If this is your name, be sure to note that. Otherwise, folks will think you were named by parents who thought you weren't going to be very attractive.

VARIATIONS: Charyn, Cheron, Lasharon, Sharnell, Sharronda

FAMOUS SHARONS: Sharon Stone attained screen fame for flashing her, um, intimate lady parts in the film *Basic Instinct*.

Sheila   MEANING: blind

{It's a good thing love is blind; otherwise, I'd have to put a bag over your head.}

GENDER: female | **ORIGIN:** Irish | **RANKING:** not in the top 1,000
ETYMOLOGY: From the Latin *caecus*, meaning blind, Sheila is not going to be a looker, and she'll probably never be able to find her car keys.
VARIATIONS: Cheyla, Shella, Shila, Shayla, Zelizi
FAMOUS SHEILAS: Sheila Blair is chairman of the Federal Deposit Insurance Corporation (FDIC). Sheila Broflovski is Kyle's mom on *South Park*.

Sheldon MEANING: steep valley

{*Well, um, son, the reason we don't come to visit much is . . . uh, the hills around your place are so steep, you know?*}

GENDER: male | **ORIGIN:** Old English | **RANKING:** not in the top 1,000
ETYMOLOGY: Sheldon began as a surname for people living in valleys with steep hills all around them. *Dun* is Old English for hill, and *scylf* is Old English for steep. It's the sort of place that will be hard to get out of.
VARIATIONS: Shelton, Sheldan, Sheldin, Sheldun, Sheldyn
FAMOUS SHELDONS: Sheldon Adelson is the billionaire CEO of the Las Vegas Sands Corporation and a man who funneled millions into Mitt Romney's presidential campaign.

Sherman MEANING: shear man

{*At least he's really good at running with scissors.*}

GENDER: male | **ORIGIN:** English | **RANKING:** not in the top 1,000
ETYMOLOGY: At one time, cloth cutters were not children working in sweat shops for pennies a day. Being a sherman, or cloth cutter, was a skilled profession. It became a last name and later a first name. Parents probably choose the name because it sounds "manly," evoking Sherman tanks and Sherman's March to the Sea. Instead, it should suggest such, um, less-manly associations as *Project Runway*.

VARIATIONS: Scherman, Schermann, Shearman, Shermaine, Shermann

FAMOUS SHERMANS: Sherman Hemsley (1938–2012) is an actor best known for his roles as George Jefferson in *The Jeffersons* and as Deacon Ernest Frye on *Amen*. Sherman Alexie is a Native-American author whose first book of short stories was titled *The Lone Ranger and Tonto Fistfight in Heaven*.

Simon   MEANING: he who hears

{*I don't care* what *your name is. You may hear me, but you never* listen!}

GENDER: male | **ORIGIN:** Hebew | **RANKING:** 256

ETYMOLOGY: *Simon* is Hebrew for he who hears, as in hears the Word of God. Simon also probably hears dead people. Pretty creepy!

VARIATIONS: Samien, Shimmel, Simeon, Simmon, Zimon

FAMOUS SIMONS: From 2001 to 2010, Simon Cowell terrorized wannabe professional singers on *American Idol*. Simon Wiesenthal (1908–2005) survived Nazi concentration camps and devoted the rest of his life to tracking down fugitive Nazis.

Skip   MEANING: skipper

{*Skip, Muffy, and Archibald are such adorable little parvenus!*}

GENDER: male | **ORIGIN:** English | **RANKING:** not in the top 1,000

ETYMOLOGY: Skip is short for skipper, the captain of a ship. This is a popular name for lower-middle-class parents who want their children to sound upper middle class. For God's sake, "skip" is something one does "to my lou," whatever that means. It's a name one might give a jaunty pet poodle. Your kid's nickname will be the same as a brand of peanut butter! Skippy is not a name anyone can take seriously!

VARIATIONS: Skipp, Skipper, Skippie, Skyp, Skyppe

Sky **MEANING:** sky

{*Welcome to the "My Parents Were Wannabe Hippies" Convention, Sky!*}

GENDER: unisex, typically female | **ORIGIN:** American | **RANKING:** not in the top 1,000

ETYMOLOGY: The sky can be beautiful. It can also threaten rain, hail, and snow. It is also remote and distant. In addition, you will be giving your daughter a perfect stripper's name. All she'll have to do is add another *y* to the end of it.

VARIATIONS: Skyy, Skky, Skye

Sloan **MEANING:** invasion, raid

{*That dude raids the fridge like he was born to do it or something!*}

GENDER: male | **ORIGIN:** Irish | **RANKING:** 889

ETYMOLOGY: Sloan stems from the Gaelic word *sluaghadh*, which means raid or invasion. Parents can look forward to more than the usual amount of privacy invasions, refrigerator raiding, and impertinent tween and teen behavior. Good times, good times.

VARIATIONS: Sloane, Sloanne, Slone, Slown, Slowne

Soledad **MEANING:** solitude

{*I want to be alone!*}

GENDER: female | **ORIGIN:** Spanish | **RANKING:** not in the top 1,000

ETYMOLOGY: *Soledad* is Spanish for solitude. This girl may not be popular, but she'll probably leave you alone most of the time. Besides, children who spend a lot of time in solitude often wind up being scholars . . . or serial killers.

VARIATIONS: Solada, Solay, Soleda, Soledada, Solita

Shakespeare Was Wrong!

Hollywood is the one place that has proven beyond the shadow of a doubt that even the Bard can be incorrect. When Juliet asks, "What's in a name," she is pointing out that Montague, Romeo's family name, is not Romeo himself. The fact that her parents hate Montagues doesn't change how sweet, romantic, and hunky her Romeo is. However, would young ladies have drooled over Bernard Schwartz? Would you like to dance like Frederick Austerlitz? Would hardcore rap be the same if the artist was Dwayne Carter? These are the real names of, respectively, Tony Curtis, Fred Astaire, and Lil Wayne. Some other surprising real names include:

- Mohawk-sporting tough guy Mr. T's real name is Lawrence Tureaud, fool!
- The scoop is that Jon Stewart's name is Jonathan Stuart Leibowitz.
- What's really scary about *Vampire Lestat* novelist Anne Rice is that her real name is Howard Allen O'Brien.
- You might want to show off your Ralph Lauren, but you probably wouldn't be caught dead draped in Ralph Lipschitz.
- Rapper Jay-Z might still be living a hard-knock life if he had tried to get famous spitting rhymes as Shawn Carter.
- Actor-comedian Redd Foxx gained mainstream success with the show *Sanford and Son*. Thus, his real name should be familiar: John Sanford.

Soren   MEANING: stern, strict

{*Please don't invite Soren. He's a total buzzkill.*}

GENDER: male | **ORIGIN:** Latin, Scandinavian | **RANKING:** 680
ETYMOLOGY: Soren is a Scandinavian version of the Latin *severus*,
meaning stern or strict. Let teachers and other authority figures be
strict. Stern-faced kids get picked on mercilessly.
VARIATIONS: Soran, Sorin, Soron, Sorren, Sorrin

Sorrell   MEANING: sour

{*Being around you always leaves a bad taste in my mouth.*}

GENDER: male | **ORIGIN:** German | **RANKING:** not in the top 1,000
ETYMOLOGY: Sorrell is based on the sorrel (note the slightly different
spelling) herb used to flavor soups and salads, and notable for its sour
taste. The plant's name derives ultimately from the German *sur*, meaning
sour. Not only is Sorrell going to have a sour temper, but too much of him
could be fatal. The element of the herb that creates its sour taste is a poison that, while harmless in small doses, can be fatal in large amounts.
VARIATIONS: Sorel, Sorell, Sorrel, Sorril, Sorrill

Spencer   MEANING: butler

{*Just let Spencer get it for us . . . like always.*}

GENDER: unisex | **ORIGIN:** English | **RANKING:** 227
ETYMOLOGY: Spencer began as an English surname, which meant "dispenser of supplies" in Middle English. It was a name bestowed upon
those who served the rich in manor houses. Gussy it up all you like, but
a dispenser of supplies is a butler, a foot servant, a peon.
VARIATIONS: Spencar, Spenser, Spincer, Spence, Spince

Stacy MEANING: fruitful

{Once again, I promise I'm on the pill!}

GENDER: unisex, typically female | **ORIGIN:** Greek | **RANKING:** 984
ETYMOLOGY: Stacy is from the Greek name Eustachys, meaning fruitful. Fruitful is good . . . if you want to be Ocotomom.
VARIATIONS: Eustacia, Anastasia, Stacey, Staci, Staycee
FAMOUS STACYS: Stacy Andrews has been an offensive tackler for such teams as the Cincinnati Bengals and the New York Giants. Stacy Ann Ferguson of The Black Eyed Peas is better known by her stage name, Fergie.

Starla MEANING: star

{I wish you were like the stars, far away and nearly out of sight.}

GENDER: female | **ORIGIN:** American | **RANKING:** not in the top 1,000
ETYMOLOGY: Starla is the word *star* with *la* attached to it. It began to become popular in the late 1950s/early 1960s, a time when the United States had its eye on the skies. The country's space program was in its infancy, and the Soviet Union offered an ever-present threat of nuclear annihilation. Then, Starla made sense. Now, it just sounds silly. Starla is the name of a favorite doll or a cartoon character, or a stripper. It's not the name of someone prospective employers will take seriously. Also, parents who name their kid Starla are kind of setting her up to fail. "Yes, sweetie you may be a star, but that doesn't mean you can win at everything. Sorry for the disappointment."
VARIATIONS: Star
FAMOUS STARLAS: Starla Brodie is a two-time World Series of Poker champion (1979, 1995).

Stockard MEANING: dweller near a tree stump

{ *It could be worse. I could've been named Dweller Near a Waste Dump.* }

GENDER: unisex | **ORIGIN:** English | **RANKING:** not in the top 1,000
ETYMOLOGY: Stockard derives from Middle English words that mean dweller near a tree stump, or dweller near a footbridge . . . like, say, a troll. Although maybe there's nothing wrong with that unless you're a billy goat.
VARIATIONS: Stock, Stokhard, Stokkard, Stockhard
FAMOUS STOCKARDS: Susan Antonia Williams Stockard adopted the stage name Stockard Channing. In her thirties, she became well known after playing teenager Rizzo in *Grease*.

Storm MEANING: a storm

{ *Don't flash your eyes at me, young lady!* }

GENDER: unisex | **ORIGIN:** American | **RANKING:** not in the top 1,000
ETYMOLOGY: Storms are exciting, yes, but that's only because they have the potential to cause massive destruction. Thus, Storms will be tempestuous and blustery, not worrying much about the effect of their words.
VARIATIONS: Storme, Stormea, Stormee, Stormy, Stormi

Sydney MEANING: wide island

{ *Don't worry, she just started doing Weight Watchers.* }

GENDER: unisex | **ORIGIN:** English | **RANKING:** 65
ETYMOLOGY: Sydney derives from the Old English *sid* (wide) and *eg* (island). Men may like their islands wide, but not their women.
VARIATIONS: Sidney, Sydnee, Sydnie, Cidney, Sid
FAMOUS SYDNEYS: Prior to the emergence of "Mayflower Madam" Sydney Biddle Barrows, Sydney was used for both genders. Since Barrows, it's used primarily for girls. Parents want their daughters to be madams, then?

Farmer, Peasant Farmer.

Bond, James Bond. He has a license to kill. Prior to political correctness, he slept with every oddly named woman (Pussy Galore, Honey Ryder, etc.) in the Western (and probably the Eastern) hemisphere. He lives a life of adventure filled with cool gadgets and amazing escapades. Originally, he was portrayed onscreen by Sean Connery, the chicest, most suave actor since Cary Grant. During Bond's 1960s heyday, the fictional spy created by Ian Fleming sold a million shaken, not stirred, vodka martinis. Most men wanted either to be Bond or *Playboy* magazine–founder Hugh Hefner. All that's well and good, but there's one significant, etymological problem with Bond, James Bond. He has a terrible name.

James is a form of Jacob, which means usurper or deceitful person. Bond is an Old Norse name that means serf (basically, slave), churl (unsophisticated yokel), and peasant farmer. Picture Sean Connery in his 007 threads. Now picture him saying, Peasant Farmer, Deceitful Peasant Farmer. Not even Britain's greatest Secret Service agent could pull that one off with savoir-faire.

Tab MEANING: meaningless

{*At least we didn't name him Afterthought or Unplanned Child.*}

GENDER: male | **ORIGIN:** American | **RANKING:** not in the top 1,000
ETYMOLOGY: A tab is something you close out at a bar. Tab is a diet soda created by Coca-Cola. As a human being's name, though, Tab is meaningless. Blame it on Arthur Kelm. No, blame it on Kelm's agent, who dubbed the fledgling actor Tab Hunter because it sounded more manly and cool than . . . Arthur Kelm. Since then, Tab has become a fairly popular name for boys.
VARIATIONS: Tabb

Taggart MEANING: son of a priest

{*Wait a minute . . . Who's your daddy?!*}

GENDER: male | **ORIGIN:** Irish | **RANKING:** not in the top 1,000
ETYMOLOGY: Taggart is a shortened form of MacTaggart, which comes from the Gaelic *mac an t'sagairt*, and means son of a priest. Even non-Catholics know that priests are (supposed to be) celibate. There aren't enough Hail Marys and Our Fathers to cleanse the sin from this name.
VARIATIONS: Taggert, Taggirt, Taggort, Taggyrt, Tag
FAMOUS TAGGARTS: *Taggart* is the name of a very popular detective television show in Scotland, which began airing in 1983.

That's a Joke, Right?

Joke names have been the scourge of bartenders and shopkeepers and the puerile domain of adolescent jokesters at least since Alexander Graham Bell invented the telephone. But what if you actually possess a "joke name"? Most likely, you would hate your parents until your dying day like the following people did:

- Anita Mann is an Emmy Award–winning choreographer who has worked with such luminaries as Elvis, Lucille Ball, and Michael Jackson. Folks who love the '80s have her to thank for the totally awesome choreography depicted weekly on *Solid Gold*.
- Phil McCracken is a sculptor from the Pacific Northwest whose muse is nature.
- Dick Swett served New Hampshire in the United States Congress from 1991 to 1995.
- Dick Hyman is a jazz pianist and composer who has recorded albums of cocktail music as well as early MOOG synthesizer–dominated records.
- Richard Face served Australia's New South Wales Legislative Assembly from 1972 to 2003. Surely the man didn't go by "Dick."

Talon MEANING: talon

{ *Maybe we should change his name to Wolverine . . . like that guy in the X-Men.* }

GENDER: male | **ORIGIN:** English | **RANKING:** 516
ETYMOLOGY: Talon is, well, talon with a capital T. Eagles are majestic (and a national symbol), but talons? They're basically bird claws. Do you want to be known as "Bird Claws"?
VARIATIONS: Talan, Talin, Talyn, Talen, Tallen

Talbot MEANING: message of destruction

{ *Debbie Downer's got nothing on you, buddy.* }

GENDER: male | **ORIGIN:** German | **RANKING:** not in the top 1,000
ETYMOLOGY: Talbot is made up of two Germanic elements, *tal* (destroy) and *bod* (message). That kid that all the others avoid? That kid who never has anything but doom or gloom to offer? That kid who writes bomb threats and leaves them in the boys' bathroom? That's Talbot.
VARIATIONS: Talbert, Talbott, Tallbot, Tallbott, Tallie
FAMOUS TALBOTS: Talbot is more common as a surname than as a given name. One Talbot who brought destruction is fictional Larry Talbot, the occasionally hairy protagonist of *The Wolf Man*.

Talia MEANING: dew from God

{ *Oh man, I got Talia all over my shoes!* }

GENDER: female | **ORIGIN:** Hebrew | **RANKING:** 431
ETYMOLOGY: Dew from God? Technically, anything from God is a gift. But dew? That's the stuff that soaks your socks on your way out to snag the morning paper. And if rain is God's tears, as some parents tell their children, then what is dew? God's sweat? Eew. That's just gross.
VARIATIONS: Talya, Thalia, Tahlea, Talaya, Talea

Tanner MEANING: leather maker

{I'm going to tan your hide, young man!}

GENDER: male | **ORIGIN:** English | **RANKING:** 182

ETYMOLOGY: Tanner began as an English surname for folks who tanned hides. At first, "leather maker" may sound cool. But think about it. To make leather, you've got to kill, then skin, an animal. Then you've got to remove flesh, fat, and hair from the skin using tannin (a bitter astringent found in some bark) or other acidic compounds. The bottom line: Making leather is gross. Tanner is gross.

VARIATIONS: Tanar, Taner, Tannar, Tannere, Thanner

Tariq MEANING: one who pounds at the door

{Knock! Knock! Who's there? Tariq! Knock! Knock! Who's there? Tariq! Knock! Knock! Who's there? Tariq!}

GENDER: male | **ORIGIN:** Arabic | **RANKING:** not in the top 1,000

ETYMOLOGY: Tariq derives from the Arabic *taraqa*, the name for the "morning star," i.e., the planet Venus. *Taraqa* translates to "the one who pounds at the door" because the morning star is the first to brighten the sky and wake people up. Parents lose all privacy anyway, so if you're looking for some pounding at the door when you and your mate are hoping for some "intimate time" or even just alone time, Tariq is the name you're looking for.

VARIATIONS: Tareq, Taryq, Taryque, Tarac, Tarik

FAMOUS TARIQS: Tariq Aziz was a close associate of Iraqi president Saddam Hussein and served as his deputy prime minister from 1979 to 2003. He remains in prison in Baghdad.

Joined in Holy Terrible Name Matrimony

Ah, wedded bliss. Two people meet (probably online these days), fall in love, and dream of a future filled with success and babies. One thing they may not pay attention to—until it shows up in the local paper's wedding announcements—is the combination of their last names. Maybe they should. Huffingtonpost.com combed the nation's newspapers and found some epic wedding announcement fails. Some of the best follow.

- Best-Lay (Jennifer Lynn Lay and William Daniel Best of Maryville, Tennessee)
- Speedy-Zieper (Brenda Ann Speedy and Scott Zieper of Denver, Colorado)
- Partee-Moore (Lauren Elizabeth Partee of Mountain Home, Arkansas, and William Allen Moore of Ash Flat, Arkansas)
- Moore-Bacon (Amy Michelle Moore and Anthony Edward Bacon of Leland, North Carolina)
- Long-Wiwi (Kelly Ann Long and Eric Paul Wiwi of Liberty, Indiana)
- Looney-Warde (Shelby Warde of Salem, Oregon, and Joe Looney of Prineville, Oregon)
- Gorey-Butcher (Kara Sue Gorey and John Charles Butcher, Jr., of Lubbock, Texas)

Taurus   MEANING: bull

{*You're the most stubborn man I've ever met, and I wish I knew why!*}

GENDER: male | **ORIGIN:** Latin | **RANKING:** not in the top 1,000
ETYMOLOGY: *Taurus* is Latin for bull, but the name is based typically on the zodiacal sign. If you choose this name, you're announcing to the world, "Our baby was conceived between April 19 and May 20!" Talk about TMI! In addition, bulls are notable for stubbornness, for being killed by guys in spangly costumes who wave capes, and for not winning an NBA championship since Michael Jordan "retired" in 1998 (he "unretired" himself with the Washington Wizards in 2001).
VARIATIONS: Taurean, Taurin, Taurino, Tauris, Toro

Terra   MEANING: dirt

{*Behave, Terra, so we don't always have to be so firm with you!*}

GENDER: female | **ORIGIN:** Latin | **RANKING:** not in the top 1,000
ETYMOLOGY: *Terra* is Latin for earth, ground, or land. In a word: dirt. Parents who name their daughter dirt are probably going for Tara, as in bad actress Tara Reid or as in Scarlett O'Hara's ancestral home. Tara comes from Gaelic words that mean tower or hill. Be kind. Don't name your child after dirt.
VARIATIONS: Tera, Terah, Terenah, Terre, Tiera

Terrell   MEANING: stubborn

{*Terrell, most mules are more compliant than you!*}

GENDER: male | **ORIGIN:** French | **RANKING:** 621
ETYMOLOGY: Terrell derives from the Old French word *tirel*, which means to pull. It was used as slang for stubborn people. So if little Terrell refuses to drink his bottle, sleep through the night, do his home-

work, take out the trash, date a girl of whom you approve, go to college, or move out of your basement, then you have only yourself—and your poor choice of name—to blame.

VARIATIONS: Tyrel, Taral, Tarell, Terril, Teryl

Terrence MEANING: instigator

{*But Terrence told me to eat bananas and chug Sprite! How was I supposed to know it would make me throw up all over Mrs. Tanenbaum?*}

GENDER: male | **ORIGIN:** Greek, Irish | **RANKING:** 646

ETYMOLOGY: Terrence is an Anglicized version of the Gaelic name Toirdhealbhach (say that three times fast). That name derives from the Greek *toirdhealbh*, which means instigator. Thus, little Terrence will be a future Eddie Haskell. If you're too young to know the reference, Haskell was on an old television show called *Leave It to Beaver*. He was a kid who would act like a sycophant toward parents while, in the background, he would get his friends to do things that would get them in trouble. Thus, they got in trouble and Haskell didn't. A charitable description of someone named Terrence is pot-stirrer.

VARIATIONS: Terence, Terance, Tarrance, Torrence, Terry

Terry MEANING: stubborn

{*I don't want to go to bed, and you can't make me!*}

GENDER: unisex | **ORIGIN:** French | **RANKING:** 536

ETYMOLOGY: Terry stems from the Old French word *tirer*, which means to pull, suggesting a stubborn nature. Get used to lots of stomped feet, temper tantrums, and willful exchanges with little Terry!

VARIATIONS: Thierry, Tery, Terrey, Teri, Teree

FAMOUS TERRYS: Terry Gilliam was the American-born member of the Monty Python comedy troupe. Terry Bollea is better known by his nom-de-ring, Hulk Hogan.

Tessa MEANING: fifth-born daughter

{*Damn it! Are we ever going to get a son?!*}

GENDER: female | **ORIGIN:** Latin | **RANKING:** 229

ETYMOLOGY: Tessa is a diminutive of several names, including Quintella, Latin for fifth daughter, which makes sense if Tessa *is* your fifth-born daughter. Otherwise, the name is nonsense and suggests she's just not your favorite.

VARIATIONS: Theresa, Teresa, Tess, Taesha, Tajsee

FAMOUS TESSAS: Tessa Bonhomme won an Olympic Gold Medal in women's hockey at the 2010 Vancouver Olympics.

Tex MEANING: Texas, y'all

{*Tex, I'm afraid we're going to have to give you the boot.*}

GENDER: unisex | **ORIGIN:** American | **RANKING:** not in the top 1,000

ETYMOLOGY: All residents must have some amount of pride in their state, but Texas pride is fetishistic. You won't see little Del (short for Delaware) crawling around or Neb (Nebraska) or Dak (North or South Dakota). If you come across Al, it's not short for Alabama or Alaska. Flo is Florence, not Florida. Ida is Ida . . . not Idaho. Get over yourself, Lone Star State.

VARIATIONS: Tejas, Texas, Texen, Texon, Texx

FAMOUS TEXES: *Tex* is the fourth novel by S. E. (Susan Eloise) Hinton, best known for her first novel, *The Outsiders*.

Thor MEANING: thunder

{*I've got a headache, Thor. Can you do your incessant hammering later?*}

GENDER: male | **ORIGIN:** Norse, Marvel Comics | **RANKING:** not in the top 1,000

ETYMOLOGY: *Thor* is Old Norse for thunder. Why would you want to name your child for thunder? It's loud, and it makes your dog whine and crawl into the bathtub. And while Thor lent his name to one of our days of the week (Thursday), Thor is best known as a flaxen-haired, hammer-wielding denizen of comic books and the silver screen. What are you going to name the other kids? Spider-Man? Silver Surfer? Mr. Fantastic? Actually, that one's kind of cool . . .

VARIATIONS: Thore, Tor

FAMOUS THORS: Thor is an Iowa town with fewer than 200 residents. Well, it's famous to them.

Trace MEANING: warlike

{ *Give me the remote, or I'll go to DEFCON 2!* }

GENDER: male | **ORIGIN:** Irish | **RANKING:** 577

ETYMOLOGY: Trace is a short form of Tracy, which is from the Gaelic *treasach* meaning warlike. Don't mess with Trace!

VARIATIONS: Tracy, Tracea, Tracee, Traci, Tracey

FAMOUS TRACES: Comedian Tracy Morgan went from *Saturday Night Live* cast member to a recurring role on *30 Rock*. British comedienne Tracey Ullman's popular variety show spawned *The Simpsons* in 1989.

Travis MEANING: toll collector

{ *He's so cute when he forces other kids to give him their lunch money before he lets them enter the bathroom!* }

GENDER: male | **ORIGIN:** French | **RANKING:** 191

ETYMOLOGY: From the Old French word *traverser*, meaning to cross, Travis was at first a last name used for toll collectors. Even if you have E-ZPass, you hate toll collectors. You know you do.

VARIATIONS: Travais, Travers, Traves, Travious, Trevys

Trent MEANING: invader, trespasser

{It came down to Peeping Tom or Trent. We went with Trent. }

GENDER: male | **ORIGIN:** Irish, English | **RANKING:** 373
ETYMOLOGY: Trent is based on England's Trent River. The meaning of Trent is disputed, but the most likely etymology is that the name comes from Gaelic words *tros* (over) and *hynt* (way). The idea was that the Trent River floods so much that it invades or trespasses over the land through which it flows. It goes boldly to places where it doesn't belong. The bottom line: You might as well just name your kid Interloper.
VARIATIONS: Trenton, Trente, Trentin, Trint, Trynte

Trista MEANING: sad

{Well, she's never going to be Little Miss Sunshine. }

GENDER: female | **ORIGIN:** Latin | **RANKING:** not in the top 1,000
ETYMOLOGY: Trista is from the Latin *tristis*, meaning sad. 'Nuff said.
VARIATIONS: Tristah, Tristana, Tristen, Tristessa, Trysta
FAMOUS TRISTAS: Trista Rehn was a runner-up during the first season of reality television's *The Bachelor*. In 2003, she became the star of spinoff *The Bachelorette*.

Tristan MEANING: tumult, riot

{He said his first word and got the first item on his rap sheet today! }

GENDER: male, occasionally female | **ORIGIN:** Irish | **RANKING:** 87
ETYMOLOGY: So you want a little hellion, do you? Well, you've picked the right name. Tristan stems from the Celtic *drest*, which means riot, tumult, din, anarchy, etc. When you go on vacation and leave him at home, don't be surprised when he takes all the food money, uses it to buy beer at that place that never cards anybody, invites all his friends

over, and totally wrecks your house until annoyed neighbors involve the local authorities. That's just Tristan. You made him what he is, starting with his name. Deal with it.

VARIATIONS: Trestan, Trestin, Tristram, Tryston, Trystan

Twyla MEANING: twilight

{*Twyla, you suck . . . and I'm not talking about vampires!*}

GENDER: female | **ORIGIN:** English | **RANKING:** not in the top 1,000
ETYMOLOGY: Twyla is a derivative of twilight. Twilight can be a pleasant time of the day, but it's also an indecisive period, not quite day and not quite night. Thus, Twyla will take forever to make any choice, be it ice cream flavor or china pattern. In addition, the name Twyla became popular in the late nineteenth century and pretty much dropped off the map by the 1970s . . . until the last few years. The most likely reason is that people are naming their daughters after that "vampire love" series by Stephenie Meyer. Giving a child this name is like getting a tattoo; it's cool at the time, but it's horribly embarrassing years later.

VARIATIONS: Twila, Twilah, Twilla, Twylah, Twylla
FAMOUS TWYLAS: Twyla Tharp is a famous dancer and choreographer.

Tyler MEANING: tiler of roofs

{*As soon as he gets out of diapers, we're going to see if he can fix that hole in the roof.*}

GENDER: unisex | **ORIGIN:** English | **RANKING:** 38
ETYMOLOGY: Tyler began as an English surname for people who tiled roofs. Tiling roofs is a fine profession. Except for the heat. And the bugs. And the danger. And the probability of working for a shady contractor who pays you in cash and laughs at questions about health insurance. If you're lucky, you might get workman's comp.

VARIATIONS: Tielar, Tieler, Tielor, Tylor, Ty

Tawdry Audrey

Audrey means noble strength, and it evokes the beautiful, willowy Audrey Hepburn of classic screen. In short, there's nothing tawdry about Audrey . . . or so you'd think. In fact, the word tawdry, meaning cheap and gaudy, owes its origin to Audrey and to those fun-killers of old, the Puritans.

St. Audrey (636–679) married twice, but she determined prior to her marriages that she would maintain a lifelong vow of virginity. In those days, women didn't have much say in matrimonial matters. Ultimately, she managed to become a nun, despite efforts by her second husband to consummate their marriage by force. Later, Audrey founded a monastery in the English town of Ely.

Some 1,000 years later, Ely locals established an annual fair in honor of St. Audrey. Lacework was a popular item sold at the fair. The Puritans, who disliked ornamentation of any kind except for scarlet letters on fallen women, disliked the lacework, considering it cheap and gaudy. Through Puritan disdain and an etymological shift, St. Audrey became tawdry.

U & V

Upton   MEANING: upper town

{ *We think that sounds so much cooler than Suburbs.* }

GENDER: male | **ORIGIN:** English | **RANKING:** not in the top 1,000
ETYMOLOGY: Upton derives from an Old English place name meaning upper town. At least you'll know that Upton's from the right side of the tracks . . . even if he's a total snob.
VARIATIONS: Uptan, Upten, Uptown, Uptun
FAMOUS UPTONS: Upton Sinclair (1878–1968) is best known for his novel *The Jungle* (1906), which exposed disgusting conditions in the United States meatpacking industry, and led to government reform.

Ursula   MEANING: little female bear

{ *She's little, but she'll gnaw your legs off when she's hungry.* }

GENDER: female | **ORIGIN:** Latin | **RANKING:** not in the top 1,000
ETYMOLOGY: *Ursa* is Latin for female bear, and the *la* at the end means little. Little female bear? Not hot. Little female bear? Looks cute but can rip your lungs out.
VARIATIONS: Irsaline, Orsa, Ursala, Ursola, Urzulla
FAMOUS URSULAS: The quintessential Ursula remains 1960s screen siren Ursula Andress. The statuesque, well-endowed Swiss beauty left (male portions of) audiences breathless when she emerged, skimpy-white-bikini-clad, from the sea in the original James Bond film, *Dr. No.* She is probably what parents have in mind when they choose this name.

Vachel MEANING: cow herd

{What's that on your shoes, Vachel?}

GENDER: male | **ORIGIN:** French | **RANKING:** not in the top 1,000
ETYMOLOGY: Vachel is a dashing, poetic name, just right for, say, the befanged protagonist of a paranormal romance novel. The name's meaning, however, is far from lyrical. Vachel comes from *vacher*, French for cowherd. Of course, cowboys have their own mystique and have been the cause of buxom bosom–heaving in many other types of romance novels. But in real life, cowboys are probably sweaty, dirty, smelly, and covered in cow dung.
VARIATIONS: Vache, Vachele, Vachell, Vishal, Vogel
FAMOUS VACHELS: Poet Nicholas Vachel Lindsay (1879–1931) went by his middle name. Though not a cowherd, the Midwesterner did write many poems of the prairies, which he often sang. He was thus called the Prairie Troubador.

Vaughn MEANING: little, small

{Vaughn, would you please stand up? Oh, you are standing.}

GENDER: unisex, typically male | **ORIGIN:** Welsh | **RANKING:** 903
ETYMOLOGY: Vaughn stems from the Welsh word *bychan*, which means small, little, tiny, petite, minute, undersized, shrimpy, insignificant, etc. Get the picture?
VARIATIONS: Vaughan, Vaune, Vawn, Vawne, Von

Vega MEANING: swooping vulture

{What do you mean I can't bring my carrion luggage on the plane?}

GENDER: unisex | **ORIGIN:** Arabic | **RANKING:** not in the top 1,000
ETYMOLOGY: *Vega* is Arabic for swooping vulture. It's highly unlikely

that you'll find a Vega who's a vegetarian. She's a carnivore through and through.

VARIATIONS: Vaga, Vegas, Vagish, Vasu, Viggo

FAMOUS VEGAS: Singer-composer Suzanne Vega achieved fame in the 1980s for two of her songs: "Luka" and "Tom's Diner."

Viggo   MEANING: warlike

{Viggo can smart bomb his diaper like no other kid!}

GENDER: male | **ORIGIN:** Norse | **RANKING:** 32 in Sweden; not in the top 1,000 in the United States

ETYMOLOGY: You want a boy who will stand up for himself, but you don't want one who doesn't know how to choose his battles. Little Viggo will argue about bath time, bedtime, eating veggies, doing his chores . . . in short, everything. Raising kids is enough work, so why make the job even harder?

VARIATIONS: Vego, Vig, Vigo, Vagas, Vagish

Virgil   MEANING: virgin

{Dude, tell anyone what my names means, and I'll kill you.}

GENDER: male | **ORIGIN:** Latin | **RANKING:** not in the top 1,000

ETYMOLOGY: Virgil derives from the Latin *virgo*, meaning maiden. Maiden is a nice way to say virgin. If you're a guy, you will want your friends to believe you lost your virginity by age eleven. Otherwise, you will hear jokes about being a "40-year-old virgin" until you want to swallow cyanide.

VARIATIONS: Vergil, Virgillo

FAMOUS VIRGILS: Music runs through Virgils's veins. Virgil Donati is an Australian drummer. Virgil Moorfield is an American drummer. And Virgil Thompson is an American composer.

Pagan Months

If you've never taken the time to think about where our months got their names, all you have to do is look to Rome. In 46 B.C.E., Julius Caesar revamped the original ten-month Roman calendar, leading to the Julian calendar we have today.

- **January:** Janus was the Roman god of gates and doorways and seemed an appropriate figure with which to begin the year.
- **February:** Februa was a Roman festival of purification.
- **March:** March is named for Mars, the Roman god of war.
- **April:** April is named for Aphrodite, the Roman goddess of love.
- **May:** May is named for Maia, a Roman goddess who symbolized growth.
- **June:** June is named for Juno, wife (and sister!) of Jupiter.
- **July:** Julius Caesar revamped the calendar, so he named one of the months, July, after himself.
- **August:** Augustus Caesar made a few alterations to the calendar and named a month after himself.
- **September/October/November/December:** September (seventh month), October (eighth month), November (ninth month), and December (tenth month) hark back to the pre-Julian ten-month calendar, which helps explain why they aren't actually the seventh, eighth, ninth, and tenth months of the year.

Walker MEANING: cloth fuller

{ Hmm. People may not know what a "cloth fuller" is, so maybe we should just name him Sweatshop Worker. }

GENDER: male | **ORIGIN:** English | **RANKING:** 417

ETYMOLOGY: Walker is from an Old English word, *wealcan*, which means walk. But the name Walker was used initially as the last name of a cloth fuller. A cloth fuller's job was to walk on wool in order to clean and thicken it. Except for the fact that this job was probably done outdoors, Walker has a lot in common with today's sweatshop worker.

VARIATIONS: Wakker, Walk, Walkar, Walkir, Walkor

Wallace MEANING: foreigner

{ We can't understand why our little boy just never fits in anywhere. }

GENDER: male | **ORIGIN:** French | **RANKING:** not in the top 1,000

ETYMOLOGY: Wallace stems from the Norman French word *waleis* meaning Welsh or foreigner. And we all know humanity has a great history of welcoming strangers peacefully into their communities without prejudice or fear . . . right? Hey, maybe he'll have a gift for languages?

VARIATIONS: Wallis, Walsh, Welsh, Wallach, Wally

FAMOUS WALLACES: Wallace Beery (1885–1949) was a popular actor who starred in more than 250 roles. Wallace Stevens (1879–1955) was an insurance executive who moonlighted as one of America's best poets.

Mythological Names

Mythology has been popular for thousands of years, and it continues to find its way into popular culture via lousy remakes of lousy movies (*Clash of the Titans*) and via a series of books for teens (Rick Riordan's *Percy Jackson & the Olympians* series).

Some mythologically based names remain popular. Chloe, for example, means green shoot and was one of the epithets for the Greek agriculture goddess, Demeter. Other names . . . well, you aren't likely to see them in real life.

- Aegle was a character who played bit parts in Greek myths. Her name means radiance or glory.
- Agrona was a Celtic goddess of war and death. Her name means battle or slaughter.
- Balder was a figure in Norse mythology. A son of the god Odin, Balder's name means prince. Balder was killed by, of all things, a sprig of mistletoe.
- Elpis means hope in Greek. When Pandora opened her jar and unleashed anarchy into the world, Elpis—the personification of hope—was the last item left in the jar.
- Frigg means beloved in Old Norse. She was the Norse goddess of the Earth and Odin's wife. She also lends her name to Friday, everyone's favorite weekday.

Warren MEANING: animal enclosure

{I just feel trapped in this relationship, Warren.}

GENDER: male | ORIGIN: French | RANKING: 501
ETYMOLOGY: The name Warren comes from the Old French *warrene*, meaning animal enclosure. Perhaps you've heard of a rabbit warren. It's a cage for rabbits. Rabbits stay in them until they are killed for meat or fur. That's right. Anyone named Warren has been named after death row for cute, fluffy bunnies.
VARIATIONS: Waran, Waren, Warran, Warrin, Worrin

Wayne MEANING: wagon maker

{Maker Of Stuff We No Longer Need just had too negative a ring to it, so we went with Wayne.}

GENDER: male | ORIGIN: English | RANKING: 704
ETYMOLOGY: Wayne is from the Old English word *waegn*, meaning wagon or cart. Initially, it was a surname for folks who made carts and wagons. In effect, you're naming your son Obsolete. Landlines for telephones, cameras that use actual film, encyclopedias found between book covers, and horse-drawn wagons. You're "waning" your child's future before he gets a chance to screw it up himself.
VARIATIONS: Waen, Waene, Wain, Wane, Wayn

Wendell MEANING: wanderer, Vandal

{We're naming the next one Tasmanian Devil.}

GENDER: male | ORIGIN: German | RANKING: not in the top 1,000
ETYMOLOGY: Wendell evokes a 98-pound weakling, but the name's origin should strike fear into hearts. Wendell derives from *wandeln*, an Old German word meaning wanderer or to wander. This word developed into Vandal, as in the group of wandering barbarians who sacked Rome in the fifth century. Their name gave us the word vandalism,

which is to destroy someone else's property. Thus, Wendell is a wandering, barbaric juvenile delinquent in training. Pray he only breaks a lamp or two when he plays in the house.

VARIATIONS: Wendall, Wendel, Windel, Windell, Wyndell

FAMOUS WENDELLS: Wendell Willkie (1892–1944) was a lawyer and dark-horse Republican candidate who opposed President Franklin Delano Roosevelt in the 1940 presidential election. He lost, of course.

Wilbur   MEANING: wild boar

{ *You smell, root through garbage, and try to hurt people when you're afraid. Sheesh. We can't take you anywhere!* }

GENDER: male | **ORIGIN:** English | **RANKING:** not in the top 1,000

ETYMOLOGY: Oh, Wilbur. Your name comes from the Middle English word *wildbor*, which means wild boar. Wild boars are ugly and smelly. Wild boars root through junk to find food. Wild boars are loved only by those who live in Arkansas (home of the UA Razorbacks).

VARIATIONS: Wilbert, Wilbart, Wilburg, Wilburn, Wilburne

FAMOUS WILBURS: Really old people will associate someone named Wilbur with Wilbur Post, a television character who played second fiddle to a talking horse named Mr. Ed. And slightly younger old people will associate this name with a pig that gets saved from the butcher shop by a spider named Charlotte.

Wilda   MEANING: untamed

{ *Where did I leave my shoes last night? And my skirt? And my underwear? Why am I naked at the bus stop?* }

GENDER: female | **ORIGIN:** English | **RANKING:** not in the top 1,000

ETYMOLOGY: Wilda derives from the Old English *wilde*, which means what you think it means: untamed or feral. If you are the type of parents who are already nervous about your future daughter's propensity for dissipation and debauchery, then do *not* name her Wilda. It's like giving her a license to act, well, wild.

VARIATIONS: Willda, Wylda, Wyllda

FAMOUS WILDAS: Wilda Gerideau-Squires is a fine-art photographer who was added in 2008 to Women in Photography International's List of Distinguished Women Photographers.

Wilder   MEANING: untamed, wild

{ *We didn't get him a playpen. We got him a dog run.* }

GENDER: male | **ORIGIN:** English | **RANKING:** not in the top 1,000

ETYMOLOGY: Wilder is an English surname sometimes used as a first name. Parents? Do you want an intractable child? Coworkers? Do you want a guy who'll steal food from the communal fridge and hit on every woman in accounting? If so, Wilder's the name for you!

VARIATIONS: Wilde, Wildey, Wylde, Wylder, Wild

FAMOUS WILDERS: Douglas Wilder was the first African-American elected governor of Virginia. Laura Ingalls Wilder created the popular *Little House on the Prairie* series.

Wiley   MEANING: fraudulent, deceptive, tricky, crafty

{ *Our neighbors had already named theirs Hedge Fund Operator.* }

GENDER: unisex, typically male | **ORIGIN:** Norse | **RANKING:** not in the top 1,000

ETYMOLOGY: Wiley basically means the same thing as *wily*; it's just that another letter has been added. Wiley (and wily) come from an Old Norse word, *vel*, which suggests all kinds of rotten things including deception, fraud, and craftiness. The good news is that someone named Wiley will have a bright future in politics or investing. The bad news is that he or she may not have a soul.

VARIATIONS: Whiley, Whylie, Wilie, Wylee, Wyly

FAMOUS WILEYS: Since classic Warner Brothers cartoons remain popular, your child will be teased as Wile E. Coyote at least until he or she begins middle school.

William   MEANING: desire helmet

{*And I desire kneepads, but we don't always get our way, do we William?*}

GENDER: male | **ORIGIN:** German | **RANKING:** 3

ETYMOLOGY: William combines the word *will*, for desire, with the German *helm*, for helmet. At least little William will always practice safe sex!

VARIATIONS: Wilhelm, Will, Bill, Liam

FAMOUS WILLIAMS: William Shakespeare wrote some of the world's most beloved plays, such as *Romeo and Juliet*, *Hamlet*, and *Macbeth*. William is also a traditional name for Great Britain's royal family.

Winchell   MEANING: from the corner

{*You can't miss it. It's the one where all the winos hang out.*}

GENDER: male | **ORIGIN:** English | **RANKING:** not in the top 1,000

ETYMOLOGY: Winchell is an English surname occasionally used as a first name. It began as a way to describe someone from a corner, or bend in the road. Just call Winchell if you're looking for a male escort. He's easy to find.

VARIATIONS: Wenchell, Winnchell, Winshell, Wynchell, Wynnchell

FAMOUS WINCHELLS: He's not a household name today, but for decades Walter Winchell (1897–1972) was a popular gossip columnist. He was the one-man *TMZ* of his day.

X, Y, & Z

Xavier   MEANING: new house

{We got a new house because we had to tear down the old one. Termites.}

GENDER: male | **ORIGIN:** Basque | **RANKING:** 77

ETYMOLOGY: This is a Basque word for new house. The Basques are a group of people who live in a region shared by France and Spain. Since most new houses currently are "underwater" and many have been foreclosed on, new houses just don't have the positive image they once had.

VARIATIONS: Javier, Zavier, Xavior, Exavier, Xzavier

FAMOUS XAVIERS: Xavier became a popular name for boys thanks to St. Francis Xavier (1506–1552), a Spanish missionary who spread the Gospel throughout Asia. Xavier was one of the founders of the Society of Jesus, also known as the Jesuits. Professor Charles Francis Xavier, AKA Professor X, is the paraplegic leader and founder of the X-Men.

Xenophon   MEANING: strange voice

{I like the guy, even though I can't understand a word he says.}

GENDER: male | **ORIGIN:** Greek | **RANKING:** not in the top 1,000

ETYMOLOGY: Maybe you want your son to sound like Elmer Fudd. Or speak with a pronounced lisp. Or slur his speech, even when he's stone-cold sober. Well, you've picked the right name! Xenophon is made up of two Greek words, *xenos* (strange) and *phone* (voice). At least he'll have a future in voice acting.

VARIATIONS: Xeno, Xenofon, Xenofone, Xenophone, Zennie

FAMOUS XENOPHONS: Xenophon was a fourth-century B.C.E. historian best known for preserving some of Socrates's sayings and for recording the life and culture of ancient Greece.

York   MEANING: pig farm

{ Nope, that's not a diaper you're smelling. }

GENDER: male | **ORIGIN:** English | **RANKING:** not in the top 1,000

ETYMOLOGY: Hey New Yorkers, you're all just New Pig Farmers! New York was named after the town of the same name in England, but the name derives from the Old English *eoforwic*, which means pig farm. Think about that the next time you're sucking down a grossly over-priced latte and getting mugged on the sidewalk by a shaky guy who needs a fix.

VARIATIONS: Yorc, Yorck, Yorker, Jorck, Yerik

FAMOUS YORKS: York was an African-American slave who was part of the Lewis and Clark Expedition.

Yui   MEANING: tie, bind

{ Naming her The Old Ball and Chain would just be too cliché. }

GENDER: female | **ORIGIN:** Japanese | **RANKING:** 2 in Japan; not in the top 1,000 in the United States

ETYMOLOGY: What does it say about the Japanese that the country's second-favorite name for girls means tie or bind? Do they hate girls? Do they think that girls just "tie men down"? Do they have odd fetishes, and if so, why do they want their precious little baby girls to remind them of these? Maybe they should consider making fewer babies and more of their stylish, dependable cars.

VARIATIONS: Ewie, Yayoi

We Need Moor Murgatroyds

Yogi Bear fans will remember Snagglepuss, an anthropomorphic feline whose favorite expression was, "Heavens to Murgatroyd." Why did he say this? It sounds funny. However, Murgatroyd is not a made-up name. According to legend, a fourteenth-century constable adopted the name, which, in Middle English, meant something like "road that leads to the moors." This was the region of which he was in charge.

Zachary MEANING: God recalls

{ *We want to return you for your defects, but unfortunately we can't send you back where you came from.* }

GENDER: male | **ORIGIN:** Hebrew | **RANKING:** 64
ETYMOLOGY: Zachary is an Anglicized version of the name Zekharyah, which means God recalls, as in God remembers. Just try slipping under the radar when you're named Zachary. Not gonna happen!
VARIATIONS: Thackery, Zacharey, Zackory, Xackery, Zeke
FAMOUS ZACHARYS: Tweens made Zachary "Zac" Efron a heartthrob after he appeared in Disney's *High School Musical*. Zachary Taylor was the twelfth president of the United States, but he died of natural causes after only sixteen months in office.

Zared MEANING: ambush

{ *We thought that Creepy Weird Sneaky Guy had too many letters.* }

GENDER: male | **ORIGIN:** Hebrew | **RANKING:** not in the top 1,000
ETYMOLOGY: You'll never know what to expect from Zared, which is Hebrew for ambush. He'll always be sneaking up on you and begging for more allowance. Who needs that?
VARIATIONS: Zaarad, Zaared, Zarad, Zarade, Zered
FAMOUS ZAREDS: Zered Bassett is a skateboarder associated with New York's famed Zoo York skateboarding company.

That's Muse-ic to My Ears

Greek mythology's muses are goddesses of inspiration in fields that range from literature to science. If you can name three or more, then you should consider auditioning for *Jeopardy!*

- Calliope is the muse of epic poetry and eloquence. Her name derives from the Greek words *kallos* (beauty) and *ops* (voice).
- Clio is the muse of history and heroic poetry. Her name derives from the Greek *kleos*, which means glory.
- Erato is the muse of lyric poetry. Her name is Greek for lovely.
- Euterpe is the muse of music and joy. Her name is Greek for delight.
- Melpomene is the muse of tragedy. Her name is Greek for choir.
- Polyhymnia is the muse of sacred poetry. Her name derives from the Greek words *polys* (much) and *hymnos* (hymn, song).
- Terpsichore is the muse of dance and dramatic chorus. Her name derives from the Greek words *terpsis* (delight) and *choros* (dance).
- Thalia is the muse of comedy and pastoral poetry. Her name derives from the Greek *thaleia*, which means to blossom.
- Urania is the muse of astronomy and astrology (once considered a hard science, rather than a hobby). Her name derives from the Greek word *ouranios*, meaning heavenly.

Zelda MEANING: gray warrior

{Gray? Not very impressive. You really need to learn how to accessorize in battle.}

GENDER: female | **ORIGIN:** German | **RANKING:** not in the top 1,000

ETYMOLOGY: Zelda is a diminutive of Griselda, which derives from *gris* (gray) and *hild* (battle). Thus, Zelda is doomed not only to be one of those annoying people always looking for a fight; she won't even make up for that with a strong sense of fashion consciousness. Go for something with more of a visual impact next time.

VARIATIONS: Selda, Zeldah, Zelde, Zella, Zel

FAMOUS ZELDAS: All roads trace back to author F. Scott Fitzgerald's wife, Zelda. A notable author in her own right, Zelda liked her bootleg alcohol just as much as her husband, and she ultimately descended into mental illness, dying in a sanitarium fire at the age of forty-seven. Video game designer Shigeru Miyamoto created the other famous Zelda, title character of the popular *Legend of Zelda* series. Miyamoto got the name from none other than Zelda Fitzgerald.

Zola MEANING: clod of earth

{Well, it's better than glob of snot.}

GENDER: unisex | **ORIGIN:** Italian | **RANKING:** not in the top 1,000

ETYMOLOGY: Zola comes from *zolla*, Italian for clod of earth or dirt. Talk about grassroots!

VARIATIONS: Zolla, Zolah, Zoilo, Zulu, Zylo

FAMOUS ZOLAS: At seventeen, South African Zola Budd broke the women's 5,000 meters world record with a time of 15:01.83, but the International Amateur Athletic Federation refused to ratify the record because of South Africa's apartheid policy.

Terrible
Names *with* Great
{*Meanings*}

The names in the previous section are common, or relatively common, names with terrible meanings. This section contains terrible names with positive meanings. Why, you might ask, are the names terrible? Well, sometimes they're appalling by association: Adolph (Hitler), Benedict (Arnold), Igor (hunchbacked sidekick in old horror movies). Sometimes they're dreadful because they sound ugly or old-fashioned (Agatha, Mildred) or wimpy (Cyril, Egbert). And finally, some are foreign names that, in their countries of origin, might sound delightful and mellifluous. In the United States, however, such names as Helga, Beulah, and Bertha sound just plain butt-ugly.

Despite the unpleasant sounds and associations of the names in this section, most have positive meanings based on their etymologies. Thus, as a public service, I offer you unusual names that deserve reconsideration.

Adolph MEANING: noble wolf

GENDER: male | **ORIGIN:** German

WHY IT'S A TERRIBLE NAME: Some dictators just ruin everything! If Adolf Hitler had been named Jack Hitler, then the world would have far fewer Jacks.

{Aw, little Adolph took his very first goose steps today!}

WHY IT DESERVES TO BE RECONSIDERED: Adolph derives from a contraction of two German words—*adal* (noble) and *wulf* (wolf)—so it means noble or majestic wolf. That's a nice, strong image for a strapping young boy.

VARIATIONS: Ad, Addolf, Addolph, Adolfo, Adolphe

RANKING: Achtung! This name is not in the top 1,000.

Agatha MEANING: good, kind

GENDER: female | **ORIGIN:** Greek

WHY IT'S A TERRIBLE NAME: The world must contain beautiful Agathas. They must be *somewhere*. Unfortunately, the name itself is ugly. Any guy being told he's been set up on a blind date with Agatha is likely to come down with food poisoning or some other horrific malady that disappears miraculously once the threat of Agatha is over.

{It beats Bagoverface, the other name we considered.}

WHY IT DESERVES TO BE RECONSIDERED: The world seems to lack kindness and goodness, so why not do your part? Agatha comes from the Greek *agathos*, meaning kind or good. Thus, even if she's as attractive as her name, at least her friends will be telling the truth when they say, "She's got a really great personality."

VARIATIONS: Agace, Agaisha, Agasha, Agatka, Atka

RANKING: It's a mystery why Agatha is not in the top 1,000.

FAMOUS AGATHAS: Agatha Christie (1890–1976) is the best-selling novelist of all time. Her various detective novels have sold more than 4 billion copies worldwide.

Adolphs Who Weren't Hitler

Hitler wasn't the only rotten Adolf in Nazi Germany. Adolf Eichmann was the mastermind of the Holocaust. Not all Adolphs are evil, of course. Here are some that have nothing to do with fascism:

- German entrepreneur Adolf Dassler (1900–1978) went by the nickname Adi, in part to distance himself from his past as an ardent member of the Nazi Party. In 1948, Adi created Adidas.
- Many millions of Americans owe their Saturday nights—good, bad, or ugly—to Adolph Busch (1839–1913), cofounder of Anheuser-Busch. Anheuser, by the way, was Adolph's father-in-law, Eberhard Anheuser.
- Let's not forget the other beer-belly baron, Adolph Coors (1847–1929). He founded his eponymous beer company in 1873.
- Wildcats aficionados still think fondly of Adolph Rupp (1901–1977). The Baron of the Bluegrass led the University of Kentucky to four NCAA basketball championships as head coach of the Wildcats from 1930 to 1972. He amassed an incredible .822 winning percentage at Kentucky.
- And finally, one Adolph left countless moviegoers in stitches, even though he never spoke a word onscreen. Adolph "Harpo" Marx (1888–1964) changed his name to Arthur in 1911. For unknown reasons, he disliked the name Adolph long before the rise of Hitler.

Agnes   MEANING: pure, chaste

GENDER: female | ORIGIN: Greek

WHY IT'S A TERRIBLE NAME: Agnes is one of those names that seems universally used when one is talking about a generic nagging wife.

{*All right, all right, Agnes. Yeah, I'll get right to my "honey-do" list.*}

WHY IT DESERVES TO BE RECONSIDERED: From the Greek *hagnos*, meaning chaste and pure, Agnes should evoke the sort of young lady parents prefer. Surely Agnes won't stay out all night with strange boys.

VARIATIONS: Aganetha, Aggye, Anesha, Anissa, Agness

RANKING: Not enough parents want chaste and pure daughters to rank this name in the top 1,000.

Archibald   MEANING: truly brave

GENDER: male | ORIGIN: German

WHY IT'S A TERRIBLE NAME: Archibald has the word *bald* in it. In addition, it's hard not to picture a CPA or some other boring, stuffy person when hearing the name.

{*We spent yet another excruciatingly tedious evening with Archibald and his wife, Hortense (see entry later on).*}

WHY IT DESERVES TO BE RECONSIDERED: Picturing an Archibald bravely leading troops into battle is difficult, but that should not be the case. The name derives from German words *erchan*, or truly, and *bald*, which means brave and not, well, bald.

VARIATIONS: Archibold, Archimbald, Arquibaldo, Arquimbaldo, Archie

RANKING: Not enough parents have been truly brave enough to make this name enter the top 1,000.

A Celebrity Menagerie

Celebrities may name their children Stephen or Lisa or some other humdrum names, but that doesn't make the news. Therefore, many choose names most people consider unique, creative, or—less charitably—irritating and stupid. For some reason, animal names are popular. Maybe these power couples are making a larger statement, equating fame with life in a zoo or a fishbowl. Or maybe they're just irritating and stupid.

- Bear Blue Jarecki is the child of Alicia Silverstone and Christopher Jarecki. Silverstone not only named him for an animal, but she (in)famously chews up his food and spits it into his mouth, like a mama bird.
- Mirabella Bunny Adams is the child of Bryan Adams and Alicia Grimaldi.
- Agnes Lark Bettany is Paul Bettany and Jennifer Connelly's daughter.
- Willem Wolf Broad is Perri Lister and William Broad's son. Broad is better known as Billy Idol.
- Birdie West DeFreitas is the child of Maura West and Scott DeFreitas.
- Oriole Nebula Leitch is the child of Donovan Leitch and Linda Lawrence.
- Sparrow James Midnight Madden is Joel Madden and Nicole Richie's son.
- Speck Wildhorse Mellencamp is the child of John Mellencamp and Elaine Irwin.

Benedict   MEANING: blessed

GENDER: male | ORIGIN: Latin

WHY IT'S A TERRIBLE NAME: Benedict Arnold (1741–1801) was
a general in the American Continental Army during the American
Revolution. Upset about being passed over for promotions, Arnold
decided to defect to the British. He plotted to turn over a fort at West
Point, New York, to the British, but his plot was discovered. Arnold
avoided capture and was made a brigadier general in the British army.
To this day, his name is synonymous with traitor.

{*What do you mean you don't trust me, baby?*}

WHY IT DESERVES TO BE RECONSIDERED: Benedict is from *benedic-
tus*, the Latin word for blessed. Your child is a blessing (until he reaches
his tween and teen years at least), so this name reflects your joy in your
baby's birth. Besides, Benedict has been the name taken by sixteen
popes, including the current one, Pope Benedict XVI (born Joseph
Aloisius Ratzinger).

VARIATIONS: Benedick, Bendix, Bendrick, Benedictos, Benicio

RANKING: Benedict still evokes "traitor" for most. The name isn't in the
top 1,000.

Bertha   MEANING: bright, famous

GENDER: female | ORIGIN: German

WHY IT'S A TERRIBLE NAME: Picture a supermodel. Now, picture that
her name is Bertha. It just doesn't work, does it?

{*From now on, please pronounce it BUHR-TAY.
That sounds much more chic.*}

WHY IT DESERVES TO BE RECONSIDERED: Bertha stems from the
German word *berht*, which means bright or famous. Who wouldn't
want his or her little girl to grow up to be bright and famous?

VARIATIONS: Barta, Bartha, Bertolda, Bertyna, Birtha

RANKING: People may want bright, famous progeny but not enough to
rank the not-particularly-euphonious Bertha in the top 1,000.

Will the Real Benedict Please Stand Up?

Eggs Benedict is not named for Revolutionary War–traitor Benedict Arnold, but that's the only thing about its origin that's definitive. The popular dish, comprised of two English muffin halves topped with poached eggs and bacon (or ham) and drenched in Hollandaise sauce, has at least three origin stories.

- **Origin One:** Stockbroker Lemuel Benedict claimed that, hungover, he walked into New York's Waldorf Hotel one morning in 1894 seeking a cure for his problem. He directed the chef to give him a meal comprised of the now-familiar components of Eggs Benedict. Impressed with the dish, the hotel added it to the menu.
- **Origin Two:** A man writing to the *New York Times Magazine* in 1967 claimed that Eggs Benedict was the creation of Commodore Elias Cornelius Benedict (1834–1920), a prominent New York banker and yachtsman.
- **Origin Three:** In response to the *New York Times Magazine* letter, a Massachusetts woman claimed that one of her relatives, Mrs. Le Grand Benedict, was the true inventor of the popular dish. According to the letter, Mrs. Benedict suggested it around the turn of the twentieth century when dining at New York City's Delmonico's.

One important question not answered by these origin stories is . . . *Does* Eggs Benedict cure a hangover?

Beulah MEANING: she who is married

GENDER: female | **ORIGIN:** Hebrew

WHY IT'S A TERRIBLE NAME: Beulah conjures up images of middle-aged spinsters with prominent facial warts.

{ I liked her online profile until I learned her actual name. }

WHY IT DESERVES TO BE RECONSIDERED: Every parent pictures his or her daughter's wedding day, and the name Beulah suggests that day will be a reality (no matter *what* she looks like). The word is Hebrew, and it refers to the Land of Israel.

VARIATIONS: Beaulah, Beulla, Beullah, Bulah, Bula

RANKING: Don't more parents want to lose a daughter and gain a son? Beulah is not in the top 1,000.

Cain MEANING: spear, beautiful

GENDER: unisex | **ORIGIN:** Hebrew, Welsh

WHY IT'S A TERRIBLE NAME: Cain committed the first murder, according to the Bible. Even worse, he murdered his brother.

{ My brother's keeper? I wouldn't let him be my parrot's keeper. }

WHY IT DESERVES TO BE RECONSIDERED: Cain can suggest weaponry, which might please fathers. Cain can suggest beautiful, which might please mothers and prospective mates.

VARIATIONS: Kain, Kayin, Caene, Cayn, Cane

RANKING: A number of parents are willing to accept the mark of Cain. The name is ranked 841.

Casper MEANING: one who keeps the treasure

GENDER: male | **ORIGIN:** Persian

WHY IT'S A TERRIBLE NAME: The name will forever be synonymous with Casper the friendly ghost.

{ The only thing scary about you is that white sheet you're wearing. }

WHY IT DESERVES TO BE RECONSIDERED: In Persian, *casper* means one who keeps the treasure, or treasurer. The treasurer has access to the funds, and he's trustworthy (at least you hope he is). Casper will have a future in banking, so don't worry about saving for your retirement.

VARIATIONS: Caspar, Kaspar, Kabar, Kasper, Kaspyr

RANKING: It's frightening—in a friendly way—that Casper is not in the top 1,000 in the United States. But it's ranked 41 in Sweden.

Columbine   MEANING: dove, a type of flower

GENDER: female | **ORIGIN:** Latin

WHY IT'S A TERRIBLE NAME: Columbine High School was the site of a deadly school shooting in 1999. Since then, "Columbine" has become synonymous with school shootings.

{ I'm skipping school. Columbine's Facebook status says she's mad. }

WHY IT DESERVES TO BE RECONSIDERED: Columbine is from a Latin word *columbina* meaning dove, and columbines are very attractive flowers. Why let a couple of teenage killers ruin a beautiful name?

VARIATIONS: Colombina

RANKING: Columbine is not in the top 1,000. Maybe it will be in another generation or so.

Cyril   MEANING: lord

GENDER: male | **ORIGIN:** Greek

WHY IT'S A TERRIBLE NAME: Cyril sounds like the name of a kid who wears thick glasses and eats paste.

{ Kick the can is boring. Let's play kick the Cyril instead! }

WHY IT DESERVES TO BE RECONSIDERED: Cyril stems from the

Greek *kyrios*, or lord. Naming your kid Cyril is like naming him Superman or Captain America, or rich nobleman.

VARIATIONS: Ciril, Cirilio, Cirilo, Kiril, Kyril

RANKING: Not enough parents want lordly children to make Cyril rank in the top 1,000.

Dagmar
MEANING: peaceful day, precious and famous

GENDER: female | **ORIGIN:** Norse, Scandinavian

WHY IT'S A TERRIBLE NAME: Dagmar evokes the opera-emoting "fat lady" of legend.

{ *It ain't over 'til Dagmar sings.* }

WHY IT DESERVES TO BE RECONSIDERED: Dagmar is a mix of Old Norse and Scandinavian words that bear diverse meanings, but they're all positive: day maiden, precious day, peaceful day, precious and famous, etc. It doesn't sound very pretty, but Dagmar is a potentially auspicious name.

VARIATIONS: Dagmaria, Dagmarie, Dagmarr, Dagomar, Dagomara

RANKING: Not enough people have overlooked the sound of the name to place Dagmar in the top 1,000.

Damian
MEANING: to tame, to subdue

GENDER: male | **ORIGIN:** Greek

WHY IT'S A TERRIBLE NAME: Even nonhorror movie fans probably think of that spooky spawn of Satan in *The Omen* movies when they hear the name Damian.

{ *Honey, did you give him this 666 tattoo on the back of his head?* }

WHY IT DESERVES TO BE RECONSIDERED: Damian derives from the Greek *damao*, meaning subdue or tame. Saint Damian lived in the third century c.e., and he is the patron saint of physicians.

VARIATIONS: Damien, Damon, Daman, Damen, Dayman

RANKING: Satan? Schmay-tan! Damian is ranked a righteous 138.

Daria   MEANING: upholder of good

GENDER: female | **ORIGIN:** Persian

WHY IT'S A TERRIBLE NAME: Daria sounds alarmingly like diarrhea.

{ That spicy squid taco gave me Daria. }

WHY IT DESERVES TO BE RECONSIDERED: Daria is one of those names that's from a mishmash of languages, but its Persian roots, *daraya* (possess) and *vahu* (good), suggest someone who will be an upstanding citizen. Of course, she might just wind up being a public defender, i.e., a lawyer who makes no money.

VARIATIONS: Darena, Dariane, Darianna, Darielle, Dhariana

RANKING: Prospective parents who want to raise upstanding young ladies have thus far refused to rank Daria in the top 1,000.

Dewey   MEANING: beloved

GENDER: male | **ORIGIN:** Hebrew

WHY IT'S A TERRIBLE NAME: The Dewey Decimal System. Yawn! The nephew of a cartoon duck with a speech impediment. A law firm's joke name, used by countless comedians: Dewey, Cheatham, and Howe (Do we cheat 'em? And how!). Dewey Defeats Truman (Not!). 'Nuff said.

{ Dewey's boring and a liar . . . when you can understand anything he says! }

WHY IT DESERVES TO BE RECONSIDERED: Dewey is a form of David, which comes from the Hebrew *dwd* and means beloved. Who doesn't want to be beloved? That would mean everyone thinks you're a great guy!

VARIATIONS: Dewea, Dewee, Dewie, Duey, Dewy

RANKING: Parents have chosen not to overlook the seamier, sillier aspects of the name and do not rank Dewey in the top 1,000.

Dorcas MEANING: gazelle

GENDER: female | **ORIGIN:** Aramaic

WHY IT'S A TERRIBLE NAME: Dorcas sounds like dork + ass.

{No, Dork Ass, we don't want to play with you!}

WHY IT DESERVES TO BE RECONSIDERED: The Aramaic word *dorkas* means gazelle. Dorcas, mentioned in Acts, is one of the few female disciples of Jesus Christ found in the Bible. So, if you're of a biblical bent and you want a daughter who'll be a gazelle on the playing field, then Dorcas may be the perfect name . . . even though kids will, most definitely, call her Dork Ass.

VARIATIONS: Dorcia, Dorckas, Dorkas

RANKING: No one wants to give their children names that are easy to make fun of. Dorcas isn't ranked in the top 1,000.

Earleen MEANING: of noble birth

GENDER: female | **ORIGIN:** English

WHY IT'S A TERRIBLE NAME: Earl, a synonym for "to vomit," is bad enough. Earleen is worse. Is it possible that there's a more redneck-sounding name on Earth than Earleen?

{Earleen just had her first date with her second cousin . . . or was it her second date with her first cousin?}

WHY IT DESERVES TO BE RECONSIDERED: Earleen comes from the Old English word *eorl*, which suggests nobility of birth, strength, fortitude, and all sorts of other good qualities that one might want in his or her child.

VARIATIONS: Earlene, Earleene, Earliene, Erlene, Irline

RANKING: Few will be able to say, "My name is Earleen." The name is not in the top 1,000.

Edsel   MEANING: noble

GENDER: male | ORIGIN: German

WHY IT'S A TERRIBLE NAME: The Ford Motor Company unveiled its Edsel division—named for founder Henry Ford's son—in 1957. The line was a disaster and production stopped in 1960. Edsel has been synonymous with "epic product fail" ever since.

{ *Poor little Edsel just can't do* **anything** *right.* }

WHY IT DESERVES TO BE RECONSIDERED: The Edsel may have had a front grille that many compared to a toilet seat, but the name's meaning has nothing to do with dubious automobile styling. It's from the Old German word *adal*, which means noble.

VARIATIONS: Etzel

RANKING: It's been over fifty years since the Edsel languished in automobile showrooms, but parents still reject the name. It's not in the top 1,000.

Egbert   MEANING: great swordsman

GENDER: male | ORIGIN: English

WHY IT'S A TERRIBLE NAME: Egbert is another of those names that evokes a wimpy kid in glasses whose ass gets kicked regularly by bullies calling him "Egg Butt."

{ *For fun around here, we just put Egbert in a trashcan and roll him down the hill.* }

WHY IT DESERVES TO BE RECONSIDERED: Egbert may sound nerdy, but the name has a very manly meaning. It derives from the Old English words *ecg* (edge of a sword) and *beorht* (bright; famous). Thus, Egbert means shining sword or great swordsman, so *he* should be the one doing the butt-kicking.

VARIATIONS: Egberte, Egbirt, Egbirte, Egburt, Egbyrt

RANKING: Cool meaning, nerdy name. Egbert is not in the top 1,000.

Most Popular Names of the Twentieth Century

Mary was the most popular name for girls for half of the twentieth century. By century's end, Mary wasn't even in the top twenty-five. The Social Security Administration, which has kept track of name popularity (among other things, of course) since the late nineteenth century has ranked name popularity by decade. The following list contains the number-one names for each decade as well as how many babies were registered with those names.

- 1900s: John (84,595) and Mary (161,508)
- 1910s: John (376,311) and Mary (478,614)
- 1920s: Robert (576,302) and Mary (701,659)
- 1930s: Robert (590,486) and Mary (572,822)
- 1940s: James (795,366) and Mary (639,902)
- 1950s: James (842,953) and Mary (625,402)
- 1960s: Michael (833,346) and Lisa (496,948)
- 1970s: Michael (707,590) and Jennifer (581,722)
- 1980s: Michael (663,322) and Jessica (469,368)
- 1990s: Michael (462,236) and Jessica (303,027)

Elvira MEANING: true to all

GENDER: female | ORIGIN: Gothic

WHY IT'S A TERRIBLE NAME: Since 1981, Elvira has been associated with a large-busted vampire who makes goofy comments about goofier movies. Cassandra Peterson's portrayal of Elvira, Mistress of the Dark, is cool—in a campy way—but she's also helped make the name akin to a cartoon character.

{*Elvira, this is Minnie, Tweety, and Tinkerbell. You should get along great!*}

WHY IT DESERVES TO BE RECONSIDERED: Elvira comes from the Gothic words *al* (all) and *wers* (true). Your little Elvira will be loyal and sweet, though she might have a penchant for cleavage-showing black clothing.

VARIATIONS: Albira, Alvira, Elveera, Elvera, Elvia

RANKING: Most parents are frightened of the dark. Elvira is not in the top 1,000.

Ethel MEANING: noble

GENDER: female | ORIGIN: English

WHY IT'S A TERRIBLE NAME: Thanks no doubt to Big Ethel, the unattractive girl who lusts for Jughead in various Archie Comic books, Ethel is one of those quintessential generic names for an unattractive girl.

{*If it weren't for your buck teeth, squinty eyes, and lack of a figure, you'd be a real knockout!*}

WHY IT DESERVES TO BE RECONSIDERED: Ethel derives from the Old English *aethel*, which means noble. Who wouldn't want a noble daughter?

VARIATIONS: Ehtel, Ethela, Etheld, Ethelda, Etilka

RANKING: Few people read Archie Comics anymore, but Ethel still hasn't risen into the top 1,000.

Fidel MEANING: faithful

GENDER: male | ORIGIN: Latin

WHY IT'S A TERRIBLE NAME: The most famous Fidel is a dictator who staged a successful Communist revolution just 90 miles from the United States. Fidel Castro made America look stupid at the disastrous Bay of Pigs invasion, and the Cuban Missile Crisis brought the world to the brink of destruction.

{*I don't care if you're a revolutionary in training! You brush your teeth, mister!*}

WHY IT DESERVES TO BE RECONSIDERED: Fidel is from the Latin *fidelis*, or faithful. Faithfulness is a wonderful quality for any human being. Be revolutionary and choose Fidel!

VARIATIONS: Fadelio, Fedelio, Fidal, Fidalio, Fido

RANKING: Viva la revolución! Fidel is not ranked in the top 1,000.

Finn MEANING: fair

GENDER: male | ORIGIN: Irish

WHY IT'S A TERRIBLE NAME: Fish have fins, and don't think for an instant that the extra *n* on the name will curb the enthusiasm of teasing children.

{*Hey Finn, wanna go for a swim? I'll just stick your head in the toilet bowl.*}

WHY IT DESERVES TO BE RECONSIDERED: Finn is from *fionn*, meaning fair and bright. The name comes from Irish mythology and the character known in English as Finn McCool. This legendary warrior had many adventures and a keen mind, but don't tell your son how McCool came to be so smart because that will return the name to lamesville. McCool spent seven years trying to catch and eat the salmon of knowledge (seriously), which gave him all the world's knowledge. After consuming the fish, McCool could regain access to the information by sucking his thumb. Yes, for real.

VARIATIONS: Fin, Fingall, Finnie, Finnis, Fynn

RANKING: He'll suck his thumb anyway. If it persists, it won't really be a problem until middle school. Finn is ranked 304.

Names That Could Ruin Your Child's School Days

When attempting to choose the right name for their baby, parents sometimes get so focused on the process that they forget the double entendres implicit in some popular names. But once children are old enough to join other rugrats on the playground, they will *never* forget this fact. As a public service, here are some reminders of names that you might consider avoiding. Some of them, however, will be found in the section of this book that deals with terrible names having good meanings. The heck with the double entendres! They won't affect you; they'll just ruin your child's life!

- Boys will dislike these names for an obvious reason: Dick, Peter, Rod, Willie, Woody.
- A john is a toilet, and it's the name of someone who consorts with ladies of the night.
- Earl and Ralph are synonyms for vomit.
- If one is Randy (for boys) or Randi (for girls), then they are in the mood for love.
- Colin (boys) and Fanny (girls) remind others of parts of their anatomy they'd rather ignore.
- And Mary Jane? Both are fine names by themselves, but together they are a synonym for an illegal herb.

Floor MEANING: flower

GENDER: female | ORIGIN: Dutch

WHY IT'S A TERRIBLE NAME: People will think you've named your child for linoleum or carpet.

{*I don't understand why people always think they can walk all over me!*}

WHY IT DESERVES TO BE RECONSIDERED: Floor is the Dutch equivalent of Flora, deriving ultimately from the Latin *flos*, meaning flower. The name is consistently popular in the Netherlands and would be appropriate for parents whose ancestry is Dutch. Besides, during infancy and toddlerhood, Floor will have an intimate acquaintance with, well, the floor. She'll spit up on it, pee on it, throw food on it, poop on it, etc.

VARIATIONS: Flooris, Floella, Floretta, Florent, Florencio

RANKING: Floor is ranked 43 in the Netherlands, but it's not in the top 1,000 in the United States.

Gretel MEANING: pearl

GENDER: female | ORIGIN: Greek

WHY IT'S A TERRIBLE NAME: Your daughter will spend her childhood fielding questions about witches and houses made out of candy. And isn't "Hansel and Gretel" at heart a story about attempted prolicide (the killing of one's children)?

{*Hey Gretel, where's Hansel? Did the witch get you yet?*}

WHY IT DESERVES TO BE RECONSIDERED: Gretel is a diminutive of Margaret, which comes from the Greek *margarites*, which means pearl. Thus, the name suggests you find your daughter a precious, rare gem and not someone you'd like to leave to starve out in the woods. Hansel, by the way, is a form of John, which means "God is merciful." So, it's not too bad a name either. If you're expecting twins, you could do worse.

VARIATIONS: Gretal, Greatal, Gredel, Grethal, Grethel

RANKING: The name isn't in the top 1,000. Of course, you rarely see any girls named Snow White or Little Red Riding Hood either.

Helga   MEANING: holy, blessed

GENDER: female | **ORIGIN:** Norse

WHY IT'S A TERRIBLE NAME: Helga sounds like it has the word *hell* in it. Besides, Helga is one of those Scandinavian names that, to American ears, sounds ugly and suggests an unattractive person is attached to it. For example, when a character named Joy in Flannery O'Connor's "Good Country People" wants to choose an "ugly" name, she chooses "Hulga," just one letter off.

{Even clock faces turn away from Helga.}

WHY IT DESERVES TO BE RECONSIDERED: The Old Norse word *heilagr*, from which Helga derives, means holy, blessed, and fortunate. These qualities aren't the least bit ugly.

VARIATIONS: Elga, Helg, Helje, Olga, Olia

RANKING: Parents can't see the holiness for the ugliness. Helga is not in the top 1,000.

Hortense   MEANING: garden

GENDER: female | **ORIGIN:** Latin

WHY IT'S A TERRIBLE NAME: It sounds like "whore" and "tense," duh!

{Isn't this supposed to relieve tension?}

WHY IT DESERVES TO BE RECONSIDERED: From the Latin *hortus*, Hortense means garden. Gardens are rich, fruitful, and productive. So what if the name sounds like a jittery streetwalker?

VARIATIONS: Ortensio, Hortensia, Hotencia, Hortenspa, Ortense

RANKING: Let's face it. This will never be a popular name. It's not in the top 1,000.

Huey MEANING: bright spirit, inspiration

GENDER: male | ORIGIN: German

WHY IT'S A TERRIBLE NAME: Huey is one of Donald Duck's nephews. Baby Huey is a giant duckling that wears a frighteningly massive diaper. Huey Long and Huey Newton notwithstanding, Huey is not the name of someone you can take seriously.

{ *Huey's such a baby that he still wears swim diapers . . . at thirty.* }

WHY IT DESERVES TO BE RECONSIDERED: Huey is a form of Hugh, which derives from the German *hug*, meaning bright spirit or inspiration. Thus, Huey should be an inspiration to others, one others will want to follow.

VARIATIONS: Hewie, Hubee, Hubey, Hughey, Hughy

RANKING: Viva la '80s! There must be a lot of Huey Lewis fans out there. Huey is ranked 896.

Hussein MEANING: handsome, beautiful, good

GENDER: male | ORIGIN: Arabic

WHY IT'S A TERRIBLE NAME: President Barack Hussein Obama has helped take the edge off this name, which many still associate with dictator and all-around-bad-guy Saddam Hussein.

{ *Baby Hussein's favorite toys are weapons of mass destruction, but it's so hard to find them!* }

WHY IT DESERVES TO BE RECONSIDERED: Hussein is from the Arabic *hasuna*, which has very positive meanings: handsome, beautiful, good. What lady wouldn't want to be with a handsome, good guy? So what if he has a name with rotten associations.

VARIATIONS: Husain, Husayn, Hussain, Haakim, Hackmann

RANKING: The Gulf War and Iraq War are too fresh. Hussein is not in the top 1,000.

Hubert etc. etc. etc. etc. etc. etc.

Who says Germans don't have a sense of humor? Hubert Blaine Wolfeschlegelsteinhausenbergerdorff, Sr., probably never did. That is the *short* version of the German-born gentleman, whose family emigrated to Philadelphia. His full name is still the longest personal name ever used. It will get its own paragraph:

Adolph Blaine Charles David Earl Frederick Gerald Hubert Irvin John Kenneth Lloyd Martin Nero Oliver Paul Quincy Randolph Sherman Thomas Uncas Victor William Xerxes Yancy Zeus Wolfeschlegelsteinhausenbergerdorffvoralternwarenge wissenhaftschaferswessenschafewarenwohlgepflegeundsorg faltigkeitbeschutzenvonangreifendurchihrraubgierigfeinde welchevoralternzwolftausendjahresvorandieerscheinenwander ersteerdemenschderraumschiffgebrauchlichtalsseinursprung vonkraftgestartseinlangefahrthinzwischensternartigraumaufder suchenachdiesternwelchegehabtbewohnbarplanetenkreisedre hensichundwohinderneurassevonverstandigmenschlichkeitkon ntefortplanzenundsicherfreuenanlebenslanglichfreudeundruhe mitnichteinfurchtvorangreifenvonandererintelligentgeschopfs-vonhinzwischensternartigraum, Sr.

Yes, he had a son who bore the same name.

Igor   MEANING: warrior

GENDER: male | **ORIGIN:** Norse

WHY IT'S A TERRIBLE NAME: Igor is the name of countless deformed second bananas showcased in horror films from the 1930s.

{*That's the wrong brain, Igor!*}

WHY IT DESERVES TO BE RECONSIDERED: Igor traces its roots to an Old Norse name, Ingvar, which means warrior for the god Ing. Basically, it's a tough-guy, take-no-crap sort of moniker that manly dads might favor for, say, the first son born after four daughters. They can tell their wives they're naming little Igor after the classical composer Igor Stravinsky.

VARIATIONS: Inger, Ingvar

RANKING: Too many people picture deformed henchmen instead of warriors. Igor is not in the top 1,000.

Jethro   MEANING: excellence, abundance

GENDER: male | **ORIGIN:** Hebrew

WHY IT'S A TERRIBLE NAME: Jethro Bodine is the name of a particularly dull-witted member of the Clampett clan on *The Beverly Hillbillies*, which continues to be popular in syndication.

{*There's not enough Texas tea on the planet to make me hang out with Jethro.*}

WHY IT DESERVES TO BE RECONSIDERED: The Hebrew word *yether*, which means excellence and abundance, is at the root of Jethro. Don't you want your son to be excellent and have lots of money so that you don't have to save for your retirement? Well, golly gee, of course you do.

VARIATIONS: Gethro, Jethroe, Jethrow, Jethrowe, Yitro

RANKING: Even hillbillies don't want Jethros in their families. The name isn't in the top 1,000.

Judas   MEANING: he who is praised

GENDER: male | **ORIGIN:** Greek, Hebrew

WHY IT'S A TERRIBLE NAME: Judas Iscariot betrayed Jesus Christ, which led some 2,000 years later to an awful film by Mel Gibson.

{*Why does that guy always want to be paid in thirty pieces of silver?*}

WHY IT DESERVES TO BE RECONSIDERED: Judas is the Greek form of the Hebrew name Judah. Both stem from the Hebrew word *ioudas*, meaning he who is praised. Someone who is sure that she's giving birth to the next Mahatma Gandhi or Martin Luther King Jr. should rescue this name.

VARIATIONS: Judah

RANKING: Few are willing to turn the other cheek and offer forgiveness to this name. It is not in the top 1,000.

Lucifer   MEANING: bringer of light

GENDER: male | **ORIGIN:** Latin

WHY IT'S A TERRIBLE NAME: Hmm . . . does the name Satan ring a bell?

{*Lucifer prefers damning strangers to befriending them.*}

WHY IT DESERVES TO BE RECONSIDERED: Why let Satan ruin a good name? From the Latin words *lucem* and *ferre* (light + bearer), Romans used Lucifer as the name for the "morning star," Venus. Then, for reasons not completely understood, early Christians began to associate Lucifer with the Devil.

VARIATIONS: no variations

RANKING: Even the Devil can't make people do it. Lucifer is not in the top 1,000.

Ludmila MEANING: beloved by the people

GENDER: female | ORIGIN: Czech

WHY IT'S A TERRIBLE NAME: Perhaps Ludmila sounds euphonious to people in Eastern European countries, but to Western ears, it sounds pretty ugly.

{ *We wanted to give our teenage daughter a legitimate reason to hate our guts.* }

WHY IT DESERVES TO BE RECONSIDERED: From the words *lyud* (people) and *mil* (dear), Ludmila suggests a young lady who will be loved by one and all . . . and not in a slutty way.

VARIATIONS: Lyudmilla, Ludmilla, Lidmila, Ludmilah, Luzmila

RANKING: Nice meaning, ugly-sounding name. Ludmila is not in the top 1,000.

Mabel MEANING: lovely

GENDER: female | ORIGIN: French

WHY IT'S A TERRIBLE NAME: Mabel sounds like the name of a waitress at a truck stop in some godforsaken state like Delaware.

{ *Mabel's high school superlative was Most Likely to Have a Crappy Minimum Wage Job For Life.* }

WHY IT DESERVES TO BE RECONSIDERED: Mabel is from the French *amabel*, or lovely. Of course you want your daughter to be lovely, don't you? Just keep her away from truck stops.

VARIATIONS: Amabel, Mabelean, Mabelline, Mabyn, Maybull

RANKING: Hold the mayo! Mabel is not in the top 1,000.

Manus MEANING: great

GENDER: male | ORIGIN: Latin

WHY IT'S A TERRIBLE NAME: Manus, though pronounced "man-uss," looks like the word anus with an *m* in front of it. Kids will find out about the spelling, and Manus will never live down his name.

{He has a great future in toilet paper sales.}

WHY IT DESERVES TO BE RECONSIDERED: Manus is from the Latin word for great (*magnus*), so you might be able to get away from the "my child's named after an ass" issue by using one of Manus's variations.

VARIATIONS: Magnus, Mogens, Mauno

RANKING: No one is cheeky enough to choose this name. It's not in the top 1,000.

Marmaduke   MEANING: fortunate, good

GENDER: male | **ORIGIN:** Welsh

WHY IT'S A TERRIBLE NAME: Marmaduke is the name of a huge, slobbery dog once a staple of the Sunday newspaper comics section. It's a name that will earn your child endless bouts of teasing in school, on the playground, and just about everywhere else. Marmaduke is a name that will make prospective employers giggle.

{Let's start with your employment history. Do you mind if I call you (chortle, chortle) Marmaduke?}

WHY IT DESERVES TO BE RECONSIDERED: Marmaduke is from the Old Welsh word *madoc*, which means fortunate or good. Headhunters may giggle at his name, but if Marmaduke does get a job, he'll probably have good luck with it. Besides, he could just go by the nickname Duke, which sounds pretty cool.

VARIATIONS: Madoc, Maelmaedoc, Marmeduke

RANKING: This old-fashioned dog name is not in the top 1,000.

Maynard   MEANING: hardy strength

GENDER: male | **ORIGIN:** German

WHY IT'S A TERRIBLE NAME: Well, it's weird and nerdy. One could blame Bob Denver, best known as the title character of *Gilligan's Island*. Before that show, Denver was most notable for his performance as stereotypical, goatee-wearing, bongo-playing, work-shirking beatnik Maynard G. Krebs on *The Many Loves of Dobie Gillis*.

{Like, wow, man, that's so heavy and far out.}

WHY IT DESERVES TO BE RECONSIDERED: Maynard comes from two German words, *magan* (strength) and *hard* (hardy). Thus, even though Maynard is, for some, a weird and nerdy name, by all rights he should be a strong and forceful character . . . who may be fond of playing bongos.

VARIATIONS: Maenar, Maenard, Maenor, Mainor, Menard

RANKING: Who even remembers *The Many Loves of Dobie Gillis*? It doesn't matter. People still hate the name. It's not in the top 1,000.

Mildred MEANING: gentle strength

GENDER: female | **ORIGIN:** English

WHY IT'S A TERRIBLE NAME: Is there a more old-fashioned name on the planet?

{Have you ever considered replacing your petticoats with a mini?}

WHY IT DESERVES TO BE RECONSIDERED: Mildred originates from two Old English words: *milde* (gentle) and *thryth* (strength). Even if she's old-fashioned, little Mildred will be the quiet type whose silence masks a bedrock of strength and fortitude.

VARIATIONS: Milda, Mildraed, Mildree, Milly, Mildereda

RANKING: Some names never go out of style, but this one does. Mildred is not in the top 1,000.

Murray MEANING: settlement by the sea

GENDER: unisex | **ORIGIN:** Scottish

WHY IT'S A TERRIBLE NAME: Murray sounds like an old guy who wears brown knee socks pulled all the way up to his knees. And he's wearing them with penny loafers that actually have pennies tucked into them. If he's not seen in advance, his name will never earn him the honor of being among the first picked for neighborhood athletic competitions.

{We'll take the sissy guy named Egbert, but you've got to take the sissy guy named Murray.}

WHY IT DESERVES TO BE RECONSIDERED: Murray is from the Moray section of Scotland. Who doesn't dream of spending their lives in a settlement by the sea? Unless it's the Arctic Ocean or the Aral Sea, which was nearly destroyed by Soviet irrigation projects . . .

VARIATIONS: Moray, Murrea, Murree, Murri, Murrey

RANKING: A few parents must be willing to overlook the old-man associations of this name but not many. Murray is not in the top 1,000.

Nero   MEANING: strong, vigorous

GENDER: male | **ORIGIN:** Latin

WHY IT'S A TERRIBLE NAME: Okay, okay, so Emperor Nero burned down most of Rome in order to clear land for his palace. And yeah, he burned Christians instead of tiki torches when lighting his backyard galas. But come on, that was 2,000 years ago. Get over it already.

{Nero bought his first lighter and took his very first fiddle lesson today!}

WHY IT DESERVES TO BE RECONSIDERED: The name Nero predates Roman civilization and means strong and vigorous. A strapping young lad your Nero will be . . . just keep him away from flammable material.

VARIATIONS: Niro, Nahor, Nameer, Narya, Nehru

RANKING: People don't give a fiddlestick about Nero. It's not in the top 1,000.

Olga   MEANING: holy, blessed

GENDER: female | **ORIGIN:** Russian

WHY IT'S A TERRIBLE NAME: Olga sounds like a stereotypical name for a spooky, weird lady who sits behind a crystal ball and reveals regrettable fortunes.

{In my crystal ball, I see you rejecting this name in the future.}

WHY IT DESERVES TO BE RECONSIDERED: Olga is the Russian form of the name Helga. Don't you want your little girl to have a blessed life?

RANKING: There won't be many Olgas in the world's future. The name is not in the top 1,000.

Onan MEANING: prosperous

GENDER: male | ORIGIN: Hebrew

WHY IT'S A TERRIBLE NAME: This passage from the Book of Genesis pretty much ruined this name: "It came to pass, when he went unto his brother's wife, that he spilled [his seed] on the ground, lest he should give seed to his brother" (38:9). To this day, *onanism* is a synonym for masturbation.

{ *Will you get out of the bathroom already? What are you doing in there?* }

WHY IT DESERVES TO BE RECONSIDERED: In Hebrew, *onan* means prosperous or strong. Giving your son this name could prepare him for a future of prosperity, and it's not going to *make* him a masturbator. He'll be doing that no matter *what* you name him.

VARIATIONS: Onann

RANKING: Guys spill their seed routinely upon reaching puberty, but none of these guys will be named Onan. This name isn't in the top 1,000.

Ophelia MEANING: profit, to help

GENDER: female | ORIGIN: Greek

WHY IT'S A TERRIBLE NAME: The best-known Ophelia is Hamlet's ill-fated girlfriend. Hamlet drives her to madness and ultimately to drown herself.

{ *I don't care if you're twenty-five. You're still going to wear water wings when you go swimming in our pool, young lady.* }

WHY IT DESERVES TO BE RECONSIDERED: Ophelia comes from the Greek word *ophelos*, which means profit or help. In other words, your

Ophelia should be an asset to any future employer. Consequently, she'll provide you with a cushy retirement on the Florida coast.

VARIATIONS: Filia, Ofeliah, Ofilia, Ovalia, Phelia

RANKING: To be or not to be? Not to be. Ophelia is not in the top 1,000.

Oral MEANING: golden

GENDER: male | **ORIGIN:** Latin

WHY IT'S A TERRIBLE NAME: First off, oral is the shortened version of a popular sexual act. Secondly, the best-known Oral is Oral Roberts, a televangelist who once famously claimed God would call him home unless he (Oral) got 8 million dollars from his followers. Amazingly, his followers raised over 9 million dollars.

{*We should have named him Shut Up Already.*}

WHY IT DESERVES TO BE RECONSIDERED: Oral derives from the Latin *aureus*, which means golden. You would, quite literally, have a golden child.

VARIATIONS: Erle, Orel, Orell, Orly, Orwel

RANKING: Apparently, enough money can't be raised to get parents to choose this name. It's not in the top 1,000.

Osama MEANING: lion

GENDER: male | **ORIGIN:** Arabic

WHY IT'S A TERRIBLE NAME: Osama bin Laden.

{*If you don't mind, Osama, I'll drive.*}

WHY IT DESERVES TO BE RECONSIDERED: *Osama* is Arabic for lion. Your son will have the strength and leadership of the king of beasts.

VARIATIONS: Usama, Ousama

RANKING: The Twin Towers still loom in too many minds. Osama's not in the top 1,000.

Least Popular Names of the Twentieth Century

The Social Security Administration has ranked the popularity of names since the late nineteenth century. Online records for older decades show the top 200 names. Therefore, number 200 would have been among the least popular baby names for each decade.

The following list shows the names in two-hundredth place, and how many babies got that name, by decade.

- 1900s: Juan (912) and Eliza (2,397)
- 1910s: Bert (4,327) and Lela (7,007)
- 1920s: Forrest (6,907) and Jeannette (9,989)
- 1930s: Alex (6,302) and Daisy (9,058)
- 1940s: Fredrick (8,228) and Stella (11,360)
- 1950s: Kelly (13,119) and Grace (15,907)
- 1960s: Herbert (13,696) and Pam (17,110)
- 1970s: Harry (11,659) and Adrienne (12,793)
- 1980s: Geoffrey (12,720) and Taylor (13,605)
- 1990s: Larry (15,942) and Mia (14,615)

Otis MEANING: wealth, fortune

GENDER: male | **ORIGIN:** German

WHY IT'S A TERRIBLE NAME: Otis evokes oafish types and dolts.

> *{How many Otises does it take to screw in a light bulb? It doesn't matter. No matter how many there are, they can't do it!}*

WHY IT DESERVES TO BE RECONSIDERED: From Germanic roots *audo* or *oto*, Otis means wealth and fortune. If you're not mercenary, then you could always claim you named him for soul singer Otis Redding.

VARIATIONS: Odis, Otes, Ottes, Otess, Otys

RANKING: No one will admit to wanting their fetus to be a nest egg. Otis is not in the top 1,000.

Pandora MEANING: all gifts

GENDER: female | **ORIGIN:** Greek

WHY IT'S A TERRIBLE NAME: According to Greek mythology, Pandora opened a box or jar, thereby releasing all the evils of mankind. Thus, the "gifts" of her name are not the kinds you want to give your granddaughter . . . unless of course you hate your granddaughter.

> *{You got that from Pandora? Well, just re-gift it for Uncle Bob's birthday next month.}*

WHY IT DESERVES TO BE RECONSIDERED: Most people have no idea that Pandora is anything other than a cool website that allows them to listen to the music of their choice interspersed with annoying commercials. Besides, the one gift Pandora kept was hope.

VARIATIONS: Doura, Pandi, Pandorea, Pandy, Pandorah

RANKING: An increasing number of people are tuning into Pandora, but they aren't using the name for their kids. It's not in the top 1,000.

Pagan Days

The days of the week pass without notice, and chances are you've never stopped to think about the meaning of the names of our days. Most of them are as pagan as a Wiccan birthday party because they are named for Roman and Norse deities.

- **Sunday:** Sunday derives from the Old English *sunnandaeg*, which means the sun's day. The Romans had already named this day after the sun.
- **Monday:** The Old English *monandaeg* translates to the moon's day and ultimately to Monday. Once again, the Romans had already named this day for the moon.
- **Tuesday:** Early Germanic tribes borrowed the Roman concept of naming days but imposed some of their own gods. German pagans also borrowed the Norse god Tyr and altered him to their Tiw. In Old English, *tiwedaeg* means Tiw's day.
- **Wednesday:** Germanic god Wodan led to the Old English *wodnesdaeg*, or Woden's day.
- **Thursday:** Thursday is Thor's day. Thor is the Norse god of thunder and strength.
- **Friday:** Friday is Frige's day. Frige is roughly equivalent to the Roman goddess of love, Venus.
- **Saturday:** Saturday retains its Roman roots. It's named for Saturn, god of liberation.

Pansy MEANING: thought

GENDER: female | ORIGIN: French
WHY IT'S A TERRIBLE NAME: Pansy is a synonym for wuss.

{*Oh, look. Here comes a 98-pound Pansy!*}

WHY IT DESERVES TO BE RECONSIDERED: Pansy comes from the French *pensee*, which means thought. Don't you want a thoughtful child? Don't you want a child who rejects the jejune and favors the cosmopolitan? In addition, pansies are pretty, durable flowers.
VARIATIONS: Pansey, Panzea, Panzi, Panzie, Pensey
RANKING: No one wants a Pansy. It's not in the top 1,000.

Percival MEANING: hard steel

GENDER: male | ORIGIN: French, Irish
WHY IT'S A TERRIBLE NAME: Some will picture a legendary Knight of the Round Table. Most will think, "What a sissy name."

{*We just didn't think Pencil Neck had the right ring to it.*}

WHY IT DESERVES TO BE RECONSIDERED: Percival stems from the Celtic word *peredur*, which means hard steel, though that word probably derives from the Old French word *percer*, or to pierce. In other words, Percival has a strong—far from wimpy—name. If—no, when—he gets picked on, he can show bullies that he's hard steel.
VARIATIONS: Perceval, Parsafal, Percy, Percyvelle, Purcell
RANKING: Egad! Percival is not in the top 1,000.

Phuc MEANING: blessed

GENDER: male | ORIGIN: Vietnamese
WHY IT'S A TERRIBLE NAME: To Western eyes, Phuc looks like a phonetic spelling of a no-no word.

{*Ah, Phuc it.*}

WHY IT DESERVES TO BE RECONSIDERED: Westerners should get over themselves and consider the actual meaning of the name. In Vietnamese, *phuc* means blessed. If you're still skittish, then consider Phuc as a middle name, or a cutesy nickname.

VARIATIONS: No variations

RANKING: Well, Phuc me. It's not in the top 1,000.

Ralph   MEANING: wolf counsel

GENDER: male | **ORIGIN:** Norse

WHY IT'S A TERRIBLE NAME: Ralph is slang for vomit.

{ *Dude, I totally just ralphed all over the bathroom.* }

WHY IT DESERVES TO BE RECONSIDERED: Ralph is the Anglicized version of a Norse name, the elements of which mean wolf counsel. The idea is that a person bearing this name will have the strength and wisdom of a wolf, not that he will be a wolf psychiatrist.

VARIATIONS: Radolphus, Radulf, Rafe, Raoul, Rolf

RANKING: Ralph doesn't make everyone want to ralph. The name is ranked 953.

FAMOUS RALPHS: Ralph Waldo Emerson embodied the true nature of his name. The nineteenth-century poet and philosopher continues to offer sage advice in his countless works.

Randall   MEANING: strong defender

GENDER: male | **ORIGIN:** German

WHY IT'S A TERRIBLE NAME: Randy is okay, but Randall—with its feminine ending—is a sissy name that your son will curse you for throughout his life.

{ *Hey Randall, you throw like a girl.* }

WHY IT DESERVES TO BE RECONSIDERED: Randall is based on the Germanic root *rand*, which means shield or any object that provides defense. Based on its origins, Randall is far from a sissy name. He's like a little Captain America, defending his corner of the playground.

VARIATIONS: Randolph, Randal, Randel, Randell, Randol

RANKING: Sissies of the world, unite! Randall is ranked 855.

Remus   MEANING: founder of Rome

GENDER: male | **ORIGIN:** Latin

WHY IT'S A TERRIBLE NAME: Older people will associate this name with Uncle Remus, a character created by white Southern author Joel Chandler Harris who was cut from the same mold as Uncle Tom.

{Please don't throw me in the briar patch!}

WHY IT DESERVES TO BE RECONSIDERED: Younger people will associate Remus with Remus Lupin, an important character in the Harry Potter series. In addition, Remus (along with twin brother Romulus) was a legendary founder of Rome.

VARIATIONS: Reamos, Reamus, Reemos, Reemus, Remco

RANKING: As Harry Potter fans age, you'll probably see this name pop up more frequently. For now, it's not in the top 1,000.

Ren   MEANING: romance, love

GENDER: unisex | **ORIGIN:** Japanese

WHY IT'S A TERRIBLE NAME: Prospective parents who grew up during the 1990s will associate Ren with an eternally pissed-off Chihuahua who hangs out with a dull-witted cat. John Kricfalusi (better known as John K.) created *The Ren & Stimpy Show*, which aired on Nickelodeon from 1991 to 1996.

{Everyone's an eediot except me!}

WHY IT DESERVES TO BE RECONSIDERED: The Japanese character for Ren means romance or love. The name will seem pretty cool as little Ren gets older and starts dating.

VARIATIONS: no variations

RANKING: Ren is the second most popular baby name in Japan, but it's not ranked in the top 1,000 in the United States.

Top Names and Their Meanings for Twins: Different Gender Edition

Twins, in general, occur in about one out of eighty births. Male-female pairs of twins are the most common among twins that are not identical. Parents of twins often like to give their children complementary names. Sometimes parents choose names that just sound good together, while others pick names that are the masculine and feminine forms of the same name. The top-five twin names for male-female twins and their meanings follow.

- Isabella and Isaiah are ranked fifth. Isabella is a form of Elizabeth and means my God is abundance. Isaiah means God is salvation.
- At fourth most popular are Emma and Ethan. Emma means whole or universal, and Ethan means enduring.
- Jayda and Jayden are ranked third. Jayda is a form of Jade, which is a reference to the precious stone. Jayden means thankful, but he probably won't be so thankful to have what sounds like a girl's name.
- Olivia and Owen are the second most popular names for female-male twins. Olivia means elf army, and Owen means youth.
- Madison and Mason are ranked number one. Madison means Mad's son, and Mason comes from the occupation.

Rex MEANING: king

GENDER: male | **ORIGIN:** Latin

WHY IT'S A TERRIBLE NAME: Rex is the quintessential dog's name, along with Rover and Rin Tin Tin.

{Rex, come here, boy.}

WHY IT DESERVES TO BE RECONSIDERED: All parents want their children to grow up and achieve greatness. They dream of future presidents, scientists, artists, and world leaders. Since *rex* is Latin for king, someone with this name will have a head start on greatness. Thus, even if he winds up no better than lower-middle management in some faceless company, he'll be the sovereign of his socioeconomic cellar.

VARIATIONS: Recks, Reks, Raj, Rakesh, Rash

RANKING: Some parents find this name fetching. Rex is ranked 617.

Rhoda MEANING: rose

GENDER: female | **ORIGIN:** Greek

WHY IT'S A TERRIBLE NAME: Rhoda evokes a hard-bitten, rode-hard-and-put-up-wet sort of gal. She's the kind of woman folks will call "ballsy."

{She doesn't just wear the pants in the family. She won't even let me buy pants.}

WHY IT DESERVES TO BE RECONSIDERED: First off, what's wrong with a tough girl? Tough girls make things happen. In addition, Rhoda should have a soft center. After all, the name stems from the word *rhodon*, which means rose.

VARIATIONS: Rhodea, Rhodee, Rhodina, Rhody, Rhona

RANKING: Parents don't apparently want tough girls with hearts of gold. Rhoda is not in the top 1,000.

Rudolph   MEANING: famous wolf

GENDER: male | **ORIGIN:** German

WHY IT'S A TERRIBLE NAME: Blame it on children's author Robert L. May. His *Rudolph the Red-Nosed Reindeer* was published in 1939. After that, Rudolph no longer evoked quintessential "Latin Lover" Rudolph Valentino; it suggested a differently-abled, ostracized woodland creature.

{Can you stick your nose under the couch so I can find my keys?}

WHY IT DESERVES TO BE RECONSIDERED: Famous reindeer aren't cool. Famous wolves, on the other hand, sound scary. Big Bad Wolf, for example, haunts the dreams of children all over the world. Rudolph derives from two German words, *hrod* (fame) and *wulf* (wolf). Little Rudolph will be the celebrity terror of the playground.

VARIATIONS: Rudolf, Rodolf, Rolf, Roelof, Rudy

RANKING: Rudolph won't be playing reindeer (or famous wolf) games on a playground near you. The name isn't in the top 1,000. Rudy, however, is ranked 733.

Sachet   MEANING: pure existence, pure consciousness

GENDER: female | **ORIGIN:** Sanskrit

WHY IT'S A TERRIBLE NAME: A sachet is that perfumed bag thingy your grandma keeps in her granny-panty drawer.

{Can you go hang out in my closet for a while? It stinks in there.}

WHY IT DESERVES TO BE RECONSIDERED: In Sanskrit, *sachet* means pure existence. In other words, it evokes an existence not clouded by the petty concerns of daily life. Sachet will be focused. She'll be on a higher astral plane than any other kid in Pampers.

VARIATIONS: Sachett, Sachette

RANKING: People are still caught up in the world of lattes, McMansions, and SUVs. Sachet is not in the top 1,000.

Saddam   MEANING: brave, powerful commander

GENDER: male | **ORIGIN:** Arabic

WHY IT'S A TERRIBLE NAME: Saddam Hussein killed thousands of his own people, and he had the nerve not to have any visible weapons of mass destruction following 9/11.

{Hey, Saddam, why are you always hiding our toys so we can't find them?}

WHY IT DESERVES TO BE RECONSIDERED: In Arabic, *saddam* means brave, powerful commander, or one who confronts. That last one is dubiously positive, but the others are pretty darn uplifting. Your little Saddam will be a natural-born leader; you'll just need to explain from an early age that tyranny is a big no-no.

VARIATIONS: Saddim, Saddum, Saddym

RANKING: Despite a massive search, Saddam cannot be found in the top 1,000.

Salome   MEANING: peace

GENDER: female | **ORIGIN:** Hebrew

WHY IT'S A TERRIBLE NAME: The seductive Salome's dance of the seven veils led to John the Baptist's decapitation. As a result, Salome is one of the original femme fatales.

{Where is your head, Salome? Oh, it's under your arm.}

WHY IT DESERVES TO BE RECONSIDERED: One bad girl shouldn't be allowed to ruin a good name. Salome (pronounced sahl-UH-may) comes from *shalom*, or peace. Your little Salome will be the family's peace-keeper, except when people mess up and call her "Sallie Mae." Then it'll be off with your head.

VARIATIONS: Salaome, Saloma, Salomah, Salomee, Sal

RANKING: People aren't losing their heads over Salome. It's not in the top 1,000.

Samson   MEANING: sun

GENDER: male | **ORIGIN:** Hebrew

WHY IT'S A TERRIBLE NAME: Samson was a hairy, strong man. He was tempted by Delilah (see earlier entry) and wound up totally emasculated, blinded, and ultimately dead. He should have tried rocking a mullet.

{*Why don't you get a haircut, hippie?*}

WHY IT DESERVES TO BE RECONSIDERED: Samson is from the Hebrew word *shemesh*, which means sun. The sun is bright. The sun brings light to the world . . . as would Samson.

VARIATIONS: Samzun, Sansao, Sansome, Sanson, Sansone

RANKING: Hey, Delilah, bite me! Samson is ranked 875.

Schuyler   MEANING: scholar

GENDER: unisex | **ORIGIN:** Dutch

WHY IT'S A TERRIBLE NAME: Your child will spend his or her entire life teaching others how to pronounce his or her damn name.

{*Samuel? Here! Sanford? Here! Shuler? Skyooler? Skoyler? It's SKYLER!*}

WHY IT DESERVES TO BE RECONSIDERED: Schuyler is from the Dutch *scholier*, meaning student or scholar. Don't you want a studious little bookworm who will earn a sweet scholarship, allowing you to take his or her college fund to the blackjack tables in Vegas? Of course you do!

VARIATIONS: Schuylar, Schylar, Skylar, Skyler, Skylor

RANKING: Sorry, no Vegas for you. Schuyler is not in the top 1,000.

Seiko   MEANING: force, truth

GENDER: unisex | **ORIGIN:** Japanese

WHY IT'S A TERRIBLE NAME: Seiko is the brand name for a watch typically associated with older people or people who can't afford to buy a Rolex.

{*What's the matter, Seiko? Can't afford* real *brands?*}

WHY IT DESERVES TO BE RECONSIDERED: In Japanese, *seiko* has several positive meanings: force, truth, exquisite, and success. Since smart phones are relegating wristwatches into the dustbin of history, these will be the only associations with the name most people would have.

VARIATIONS: Sachea, Sachiho, Sachio

FAMOUS SEIKOS: Seiko Hashimoto (born 1964) represented Japan in both the Summer and Winter Olympics from 1988 to 1996. She won a bronze medal for speed skating in 1992. Since then, Hashimoto has become a member of the House of Councillors, which is sort of like the Japanese senate. Go Seiko!

RANKING: Parents can't handle the truth. Seiko is not in the top 1,000.

Sherlock MEANING: close-cut hair

GENDER: male | **ORIGIN:** English

WHY IT'S A TERRIBLE NAME: Most people don't associate this name with a brilliant detective, despite a couple of successful movies featuring Sherlock Holmes. They associate it with the sarcastic expression, "No shit, Sherlock."

{*Brilliant deduction, doofus.*}

WHY IT DESERVES TO BE RECONSIDERED: Sherlock is from an English last name that originally meant "shear lock." Possibly, this meant the person had close-cut hair, or it might have referred to fair hair. Fair hair and close-cut hair are not awful associations. In addition, Sherlock Holmes, created by Scottish author Arthur Conan Doyle, *is* a brilliant detective.

VARIATIONS: Sherloch, Sherlocke, Shurlock, Shurlocke, Scirloc

RANKING: Sherlock is not elementary for most parents. The name is not in the top 1,000.

Shirley   MEANING: bright meadow

GENDER: female | ORIGIN: English

WHY IT'S A TERRIBLE NAME: Shirley Temple notwithstanding, Shirley is not a girly-girl name. It evokes images of tough broads. Of course, many parents might prefer a tough broad to a wilting flower.

{ *Yo, Shirley, let's go bowling.* }

WHY IT DESERVES TO BE RECONSIDERED: Shirley is from two Middle English words, *scir* (bright) and *leah* (meadow). Bright meadow is lovely, creating mental pictures of Disney cartoon films and happy, singing animals. Shirley, by the way, was once almost exclusively a male name. That changed with the 1849 publication of Charlotte Brontë's *Shirley*.

VARIATIONS: Cherly, Sherle, Sherleigh, Shirlly, Shirl

RANKING: Parents don't want bright meadows. Shirley is not in the top 1,000.

Sibyl   MEANING: seer, prophetess

GENDER: female | ORIGIN: Greek

WHY IT'S A TERRIBLE NAME: Multiple Personality Disorder will forever be associated with the name Sibyl, thanks to Flora Schreiber's 1973 book of the same name. In the book, Shirley Mason is given the name Sibyl to protect her identity. Mason allegedly had more than fifteen identifiable personalities, both male and female. After her death in 1998, some psychiatrists and psychologists have claimed that Mason faked everything, but that hasn't been proven. One way or the other, the book was turned into two films and is a classic for actresses who love to chew up scenery.

{ *Want to get away with a crime? Just pull a Sibyl in court!* }

WHY IT DESERVES TO BE RECONSIDERED: Sibyl is from the Greek *sibylla*, which means prophetess or seer. Many different countries claim sibyl legends. Typically, they are associated with holy sites, and their powers of divination are understood to be related to divine beings.

VARIATIONS: Sibbel, Sibbell, Sybil, Sable, Seble

RANKING: You won't see multiple Sibyls, probably not even a single one. The name is not in the top 1,000.

Sigmund   MEANING: victorious protector

GENDER: male | **ORIGIN:** German

WHY IT'S A TERRIBLE NAME: Sigmund sounds impossibly foreign and stodgy to most Americans. Picturing a plain guy named Sigmund is difficult. In addition, Sigmund was Freud's first name, and he will get tired of answering the question "Were you named after Freud?"

{*Little Sigmund had his first Freudian slip today!*}

WHY IT DESERVES TO BE RECONSIDERED: From *sige* (victorious) and *munt* (protector), Sigmund's meaning should suggest a strong, confident, capable human being. Unfortunately, it will probably evoke instead a bearded man with a large, phallic cigar.

VARIATIONS: Segismond, Seigmond, Siegmond, Sigurd, Ziggy

RANKING: Parents' egos won't accept this name. Sigmund isn't in the top 1,000.

Sigrid   MEANING: beautiful

GENDER: female | **ORIGIN:** Norse

WHY IT'S A TERRIBLE NAME: Despite its meaning, Sigrid sounds harsh, discordant, and ugly to most people.

{*Hey Siggy, why didn't anybody ask you to the prom?*}

WHY IT DESERVES TO BE RECONSIDERED: Sigrid derives from *fridr*, which means beautiful or fair. At one time at least, the name must have sounded euphonious. Of course, the Norsemen were not known for their heightened sense of the aesthetic.

VARIATIONS: Segred, Siegrida, Sigrath, Sigrathe, Sigryd

RANKING: Apparently, 10 million Norsemen can be wrong. The name isn't in the top 1,000.

Silas MEANING: man of the woods

GENDER: male | ORIGIN: Latin

WHY IT'S A TERRIBLE NAME: Silas will forever be linked to miserly, stingy people thanks to a work of literature imposed forcefully on generations of unwilling students. George Eliot's 1861 novel, *Silas Marner*, follows the life of its title character as he becomes a dower gent after being falsely accused of stealing from his church. Later, he becomes the surrogate father of a girl whose mother, under the influence of drugs, dies in a snowstorm. Little Eppie helps Marner's flinty heart grow by the book's end, but the name Silas still suggests an unlikeable person.

{ *Silas, your glass is always half-empty.* }

WHY IT DESERVES TO BE RECONSIDERED: From *silva*, or woods, Silas suggests an outdoor-loving, back-to-nature type. If you're a neo-hippie couple and don't want to name your child something like Sunshine or Marijuana, then you could do worse than Silas.

VARIATIONS: Cylas, Sias, Silvain, Sylus, Silvano

RANKING: A lot of parents are willing to overlook the negative associations of Silas. It is ranked 183.

Slaine MEANING: health

GENDER: unisex | ORIGIN: Irish

WHY IT'S A TERRIBLE NAME: Someone murdered has been slain. All this name appears to do is add an *e* to the word. Folks will think you have some deep-rooted, Freudian wish to kill people and play marimbas with their bones.

{ *This is Slaine, and this is our other daughter, Eradicate.* }

WHY IT DESERVES TO BE RECONSIDERED: First off, the name is pronounced "SLAW-na," not "slayn." In Gaelic, *slaine* means health. Far from wishing harm on your child or on others, you would be bestowing upon him or her the gift of good health . . . or at least that's what you could try to make others believe.

VARIATIONS: Slain, Slayn, Slane, Slean

RANKING: Too hard to pronounce. Slaine is not in the top 1,000.
FAMOUS SLAINES: Irish-American actor/hip-hop artist George Carroll goes by the nom-de-rap Slaine because it has both positive (health) and "street" (murder) associations.

Spiro MEANING: spirit

GENDER: male | ORIGIN: Greek

WHY IT'S A TERRIBLE NAME: Spiro Agnew was President Richard Nixon's vice president. Speaking of vice, Agnew resigned from office due to criminal charges (extortion, tax fraud, conspiracy). History does not look with joy on either Nixon or Agnew, who helped usher in widespread mistrust of the government.

{ *What numbskull voted to make Spiro the treasurer of this club?* }

WHY IT DESERVES TO BE RECONSIDERED: Spiro comes from *spiritus*, or spirit. Your little Spiro will have a lot of soul and be joyful . . . but he may also have more trouble keeping his hand out of the cookie jar than most kids.

VARIATIONS: Spyridon, Spiridon, Spyro, Spiros, Spyros

RANKING: Parents aren't being caught red-handed using this name. It's not in the top 1,000.

Tad MEANING: heart

GENDER: male | ORIGIN: Aramaic

WHY IT'S A TERRIBLE NAME: A tad is insignificant and unimportant: You're a tad late. Oh, not a lot of sugar, just a tad, please.

{ *This is Tad, and this is his sister, Iota.* }

WHY IT DESERVES TO BE RECONSIDERED: Tad is a shortened form of Thaddeus. Christian parents might like the name because Thaddeus was one of Christ's disciples . . . most likely. He's mentioned only in the Gospel of Matthew, replaced by Jude (not Judas) in the other Gospels. Jude and Thaddeus are, most likely, one in the same. In addition,

Thaddeus comes from the Aramaic word *taddai*, meaning heart or courageous heart. There isn't likely to be even a tad of heartlessness in your future son.

VARIATIONS: Tadhg, Tadd, Taron

RANKING: Tad remains insignificant. He's not in the top 1,000.

Tea   MEANING: gift of God

GENDER: female | **ORIGIN:** Greek

WHY IT'S A TERRIBLE NAME: Until you realize the name is pronounced "tee-uh," it looks like you've named your child after a beverage . . . and a beverage most people (except Brits) shun in favor of coffee, at that.

{We also considered Monster, Rock Star, and Red Bull.}

WHY IT DESERVES TO BE RECONSIDERED: Tea is short for Dorothea, which derives from the Greek *doron* (gift) and *theos* (god). You're showing gratefulness for the gift of your child. You're not a caffeine junkie.

VARIATIONS: Tia

RANKING: Don't put the kettle on. Tea is not in the top 1,000.

Telly   MEANING: purpose, goal

GENDER: male | **ORIGIN:** Greek

WHY IT'S A TERRIBLE NAME: Telly is what Brits call television; most British television is abysmal. Telly is also a fuschia-colored denizen of Sesame Street who is consistently in a funk. Telly Savalas was a bald actor who sucked on a lollipop and said, "Who loves ya, baby?"

{No one loves ya, Telly.}

WHY IT DESERVES TO BE RECONSIDERED: Telly may have some unpleasant associations, but the name comes from the Greek *telos*, which means purpose or goal. Telly will be a goal-oriented go-getter . . . and possibly bald.

VARIATIONS: Telly is a diminutive of Aristotle, so it doesn't have any variations.

RANKING: Parents may want a purpose-driven child, but they don't want him to be named Telly. It's not in the top 1,000.

Temperance MEANING: temperance

GENDER: female | **ORIGIN:** English

WHY IT'S A TERRIBLE NAME: Temperance is one of those excruciatingly old-fashioned names like Charity, Prudence, or Patience. It reeks of nineteenth-century Victorianism . . . or worse, of seventeenth-century Puritanism.

{ *No, Temperance, candy cigarettes are not a gateway drug.* }

WHY IT DESERVES TO BE RECONSIDERED: In today's gotta-have-it-right-now world in which people start honking at other drivers a thousandth of a second after the signal goes green, everyone's obese, and seemingly no one at all says no to drugs, what's wrong with a little temperance?

VARIATIONS: Temperancia, Temperanse, Temperence, Temperense, Temperinse

RANKING: Parents want to bring temperance back to the world. The name is ranked 941.

Uriah MEANING: God is my light

GENDER: male | **ORIGIN:** Hebrew

WHY IT'S A TERRIBLE NAME: In addition to just sounding ugly, Uriah has two additional strikes against it. First of all, Uriah was the biblical Bathsheba's husband, whom King David had killed to cover up his affair with Uriah's wife. Secondly, Dickens's character Uriah Heep is still a synonym for sycophant.

{ *Uriah's had his head up the boss' butt for so long that he's developed gills.* }

WHY IT DESERVES TO BE RECONSIDERED: Uriah is from *uriyya*, which means Yahweh (God) is my light. The idea is that your child will be God-powered, which is probably more consistent and effective than solar power and safer for the environment than fracking.

VARIATIONS: Uria, Uriel, Urias, Urija, Yuri

RANKING: More power to Uriah. It's ranked 584.

Uzi   MEANING: God is my power

GENDER: male | **ORIGIN:** Hebrew

WHY IT'S A TERRIBLE NAME: An Uzi (UZI, officially) is a submachine gun popular with religious extremists. Its name comes from its inventor, Uziel Gal.

{*The things our little Uzi does just blow us away!*}

WHY IT DESERVES TO BE RECONSIDERED: Uzi is a diminutive of Uziel, which means God is my power. Like Uriah (see previous), your little Uzi will gain his considerable (destructive) power from God.

VARIATIONS: Uziel, Uzziel, Uzzi

RANKING: There's not much of a shot at finding an Uzi on the playground. The name is not in the top 1,000.

Valentine   MEANING: strong, healthy

GENDER: unisex | **ORIGIN:** Latin

WHY IT'S A TERRIBLE NAME: Your child will be teased mercilessly every February 14th. Once he or she attains adolescence, he or she will have suicidal thoughts if caught without a date on Valentine's Day.

{*What, no date again this year, Valentine?*}

WHY IT DESERVES TO BE RECONSIDERED: Most people (with dates) love Valentine's Day, even if it is little more than an opportunity to fill the coffers of florists and greeting-card companies. More importantly, Valentine comes from the Latin *valens*, which means strong and healthy. Of course you want your child to be strong; it will help him or her get through those dateless February 14ths.

VARIATIONS: Valentin, Valentyn, Valentyne, Valantina, Valenteana

RANKING: Parents are not in love with this name. It's not in the top 1,000. Valentina, however, is ranked 153.

Velma   MEANING: will, desire

GENDER: female | **ORIGIN:** German

WHY IT'S A TERRIBLE NAME: Velma conjures up the image of a bespectacled, plain, brainy girl. You will not find an exotic dancer named Velma.

> { *Velma, we're going to rename you Daphne before you go on stage.* }

WHY IT DESERVES TO BE RECONSIDERED: Velma comes from the same root as William, *wil*, which means will, desire, determination, etc. Your Velma may or may not be a heartbreaker, but she will probably earn several patents or find the cure for cancer.

VARIATIONS: Valma, Valmai, Velna, Valena, Valonia

RANKING: Jinkies! Velma is not in the top 1,000.

Viral   MEANING: rare, precious

GENDER: male | **ORIGIN:** Sanskrit

WHY IT'S A TERRIBLE NAME: A virus is an endlessly replicating disease that can cause epidemics and lead to plagues. Or it's something that can screw up your computer, making it difficult for you to "work" on Facebook or Angry Birds at your desk.

> { *You, of all people, should know to cover your mouth when you cough!* }

WHY IT DESERVES TO BE RECONSIDERED: In Sanskrit, *viral* means rare or precious, and that's very sweet. Besides, most people associate viral with really cool videos uploaded to the Internet.

VARIATIONS: Varil, Varell, Varrell, Verel, Verrell

RANKING: Viral isn't going viral. It's not in the top 1,000.

Vito   MEANING: vitality

GENDER: male | **ORIGIN:** Latin

WHY IT'S A TERRIBLE NAME: Vito is a generic mobster name, as is its German equivalent, Guido. Marlon Brando should get the blame for this. He won a best-actor Oscar in 1973 for his portrayal of Corleone family patriarch Vito Corleone in Francis Ford Coppola's mafia epic, *The Godfather*.

{*It was so cute. Vito's first words were "mob hit."*}

WHY IT DESERVES TO BE RECONSIDERED: Vito derives from the Latin *vita*, meaning life or vitality. The name suggests a bright, cheerful child who will make friends easily . . . unless they don't think to call him Godfather.

VARIATIONS: Veit, Vitale, Veto, Veda, Viet

RANKING: Vito swims with the fishes. It's not in the top 1,000.

Vlad   MEANING: rule with greatness

GENDER: male | **ORIGIN:** Russian

WHY IT'S A TERRIBLE NAME: For vampire fans—and they are legion thanks to paranormal romances—Vlad will forever be associated with Vlad Dracul, Prince of Wallachia (1431–1476). Vlad was a brutal warrior who had a distinctive way of dealing with captured combatants; he would drop their still wriggling bodies over large wooden stakes. Death would occur eventually, but it was not instantaneous. Estimates of the number of his victims range in the tens of thousands. He gained the nickname Vlad the Impaler and was a pivotal source for Bram Stoker's novel, *Dracula* (1897).

{*You're sharp, Vlad, but I wouldn't want to stake my future on you.*}

WHY IT DESERVES TO BE RECONSIDERED: Vladimir is comprised of *volod* (rule) and *mer* (great). Thus, little Vlad will like being large and in charge, but he probably won't like garlic very much (vampires hate the stuff).

VARIATIONS: Valdo, Vladi, Vlady, Vladya, Volodya

RANKING: Parents seem to think that this name sucks. Vlad is not in the top 1,000.

Waldo   MEANING: God's rule

GENDER: male | **ORIGIN:** English

WHY IT'S A TERRIBLE NAME: Waldo is the name of a smiling, bespectacled guy who dresses like a candy cane. He gets lost in crowds, necessitating searches and increasingly annoyed cries of, "Where the *%!$% is Waldo?!"

{ *Will you please stop wandering off, already?* }

WHY IT DESERVES TO BE RECONSIDERED: Waldo is a diminutive of Oswald, from the Old English *os* (God) and *weald* (rule). Thus, even if your little Oswald wanders out in an exotic locale and gets lost, God will surely find him.

VARIATIONS: Waldy, Waleed, Walid, Walty, Waldemar

RANKING: You won't find this name in the top 1,000.

Wang   MEANING: king, royalty

GENDER: male | **ORIGIN:** Chinese

WHY IT'S A TERRIBLE NAME: In English, wang means something *totally* different from what it means in Chinese.

{ *Is that a Wang in your pocket, or are you just happy to see me?* }

WHY IT DESERVES TO BE RECONSIDERED: If you want your child to be president, then why not give him a name that means royalty or king?

VARIATIONS: no variations

RANKING: Popular in China. Not in the top 1,000 in the United States. Wonder why.

Yasser MEANING: rich

GENDER: male | **ORIGIN:** Arabic

WHY IT'S A TERRIBLE NAME: Yasser Arafat (1929–2004) was the controversial leader of the Palestine Liberation Organization. Despite being awarded a Nobel Peace Prize in 1994, Arafat was a polarizing figure. Palestinians (and some Westerners) considered him a freedom fighter, while Israelis (and some Westerners) considered him a terrorist.

{ *Um, maybe someone else should be in charge of the archery team's equipment.* }

WHY IT DESERVES TO BE RECONSIDERED: Politics doesn't deserve to put a stranglehold on names. Besides, everyone wants to make it rain—money, that is—and *yasser* is Arabic for "to be rich." Giving your baby the name Yasser will help to ensure a lifetime of financial security.

VARIATIONS: Yasir

RANKING: Freedom fighter or terrorist? Who cares?! It means money-making! The French like this name enough to rank it 475. It is not in the top 1,000 in the United States.

Yo MEANING: honest

GENDER: unisex | **ORIGIN:** Cambodian

WHY IT'S A TERRIBLE NAME: Yo is slang for "hello." It is associated with slacker teens and mouth-breathers. If you live in a Spanish-speaking community, then Yo could cause confusion because it means "I" in Spanish.

{ *Yo, wassup, Yo?* }

WHY IT DESERVES TO BE RECONSIDERED: Honesty seems, like courtesy, to be a dying concept. In Cambodian, *yo* means honest. Imagine how refreshing it will be when Yo has a kickin' party with all of his or her friends someday while you're in Acapulco and then actually owns up to what he or she did!

VARIATIONS: Yaoh, Ukko, Yu, Yuu, Du

RANKING: Yo is not in the top 1,000.

Yoko   MEANING: ocean child, child of the sun

GENDER: female | **ORIGIN:** Japanese

WHY IT'S A TERRIBLE NAME: Even though she's not at fault, many people still hate Yoko Ono and blame her for the breakup of The Beatles. For some, "Yoko Ono" is synonymous with "no-talent hanger-on."

{ These are the twins: Yoko and Groupie. }

WHY IT DESERVES TO BE RECONSIDERED: Yoko Ono may be known for wearing black and never smiling, but she had a difficult childhood. Left to her own devices, Yoko should be a "sunny" child and one who won't stay inside bugging you all the time. If you want an outdoor girl, then Yoko is a good name choice. Her name translates either to ocean child or sun child. Just make sure she never starts talking about buying a toilet for two with her musician boyfriend. Yoko and John Lennon had one of those. Ick.

VARIATIONS: Yuoko

RANKING: Oh, Yoko! You're not in the top 1,000.

Yoshi   MEANING: good luck

GENDER: unisex | **ORIGIN:** Japanese

WHY IT'S A TERRIBLE NAME: Yoshi is an adorable dragon/dinosaur who "lives" in numerous Nintendo games. You might as well name your child Scooby or Daffy.

{ Yoshi, your name is a Wii bit twee. }

WHY IT DESERVES TO BE RECONSIDERED: The Japanese character for Yoshi means good luck or righteous. Give your child this name, and he or she is sure to be lucky in life . . . and at video games.

VARIATIONS: Kiyoshi

RANKING: Eat it, Yoshi! You're not in the top 1,000.

Zed   MEANING: God's sacrifice

GENDER: male | **ORIGIN:** Hebrew

WHY IT'S A TERRIBLE NAME: In England and in many of the countries that once were (or still are) part of its empire, zed is what folks call the letter *z*. *Z* is a sucky letter because it doesn't start that many words. It starts the word zero. It's the last letter in the alphabet. It suggests someone who will always, always come in last place in life.

{ *Oh, son, you're always last . . . uh . . . first in our hearts.* }

WHY IT DESERVES TO BE RECONSIDERED: Zed is short for Zedekiah, which derives from *tzidqiyyahu*, and means God's sacrifice or God is just. Thus, your little Zed exists due to God's justice and concern for humanity. Not bad!

VARIATIONS: Zaad, Zaade, Zade, Zahed, Zaide

RANKING: Zed, you are dead. You're not in the top 1,000.

FAMOUS ZEDS: Zed is a popular name in film (*Men in Black*), television (*SWAT Kats*), and video games (*Zombie Revenge*).

Terrible
Name Breakdown

Most names found in this book are "terrible" because they refer to negative places, things, and character traits. For example, war-like tendencies, boring things, scary (or annoying) animals, and icky places. Now, I'm going to make it easier for you to find the perfect name for your baby-to-be or to find the names of co-workers or mates to avoid at all costs.

The following section breaks down many of the names in this book into categories. For example, the names that have meanings related to diminutive (nice way to say "shrimpy") size or to fierce animals or to suspect (nice way to say "psycho") personality traits.

If, for example, that guy you've just started dating seems a bit dangerous (the occasional maniacal laugh, a propensity to fight at the drop of a hat, etc.), then you can skim the entries under "Good Names for Terribly Dangerous Boys." If you find your new beau's name there, then drop him and return immediately to eHarmony. If you find yourself nodding off whenever your new girlfriend opens her mouth, look for her name under "Good Names for the Terribly Boring." At least you'll be prepared. . . .

Good Names for the Terribly Boring

- Alan
- Aphra
- Lloyd
- Narcissa
- Noah
- Rocco
- Tessa

Good Names for Boys with Terrible Personalities

- Cassius
- Cormac
- Emiliano
- Jacob
- James
- Levi
- Soren
- Sorrell
- Tariq
- Terrell
- Terrence
- Wiley

Good Names for Girls with Terrible Personalities

- Delilah
- Emily
- Hayden
- Jezebel
- Lilith
- Livia
- Reese
- Rhonda
- Rin
- Wilda

Good Names for Terribly Dangerous Boys

- Aiden
- Alfonso
- Apollo
- Biff
- Brant
- Edgar
- Garrick
- Israel
- Jarvis
- Oscar
- Sloan
- Talbot
- Trent
- Viggo
- Wendell
- Zared

Good Names for Terribly Dangerous Girls

- Catherine
- Deianira
- Kelly
- Macy
- Marcia
- Matilda
- Persephone
- Quella
- Rochelle
- Sabra
- Shae
- Zelda

Good Names for the Terribly Tiny

- Alfredo
- Avery
- Boris
- Brogan
- Curtis
- Demi
- Fay
- Gidget
- Olivia
- Paul
- Vaughn

Good Names for the Terribly Old

- Alton
- Amaya
- Kyan
- Leah
- Ola
- Priscilla
- Seneca
- Shannon

Good Names for Terribly Masculine Girls

- Addison
- Andrea
- Karla
- Leandra
- Odessa

Good Names for Terrible Jobs

- Bailey
- Carter
- Cash
- Coleman
- Cooper
- Dexter
- Fabian
- Fatima
- George
- Gideon
- Paige
- Porter
- Remy
- Sawyer
- Sergio
- Sherman
- Skip
- Spencer
- Tanner
- Travis
- Tyler
- Walker
- Wayne

Good Names for the Terribly Ugly

- Brad
- Cade
- Cameron
- Courtney
- Kennedy
- Obama
- Penelope
- Phineas
- Quigley
- Talon

Good Names for the Terribly Hairy

- Calvin
- Cassidy
- Esau
- Samson
- Sherlock

Good Girl Names for Terrible Places

- Blair
- Chelsea
- Hailey
- Lainey
- Leslie
- Phyllis
- Rhona
- Selena
- Sharon
- Sydney

Good Boy Names for Terrible Places

- Benton
- Brody
- Byron
- Darby
- Darnell
- Fenton
- Forbes
- Grover
- Hamilton
- Holden
- Horton
- Leland
- Melville
- Melvin
- Mortimer
- Ramsey
- Ripley
- Sheldon
- Upton

Good Girl Names for Terrible Animals

- Belinda
- Bernadette
- Deborah
- Ebba
- Filippa
- Linda
- Mina
- Rachel
- Ursula
- Vachel
- Vega

Good Boy Names for Terrible Animals

- Brayden
- Brock
- Cordero
- Erwin
- Giles
- Herschel
- Madden
- Ronan
- Taurus
- Wilbur
- York

Good Names for Terribly Unfortunate Boys

- Amos
- Blaise
- Claude
- Eric
- Homer
- Logan

Good Names for Terribly Unfortunate Girls

- Alexia
- Amara
- Aphra
- Barbara
- Bethany
- Brenna
- Cecilia
- Delores
- Emmalyn
- Enola
- Giselle
- Letha
- Linda
- Mallory
- Mara
- Mary
- Ophelia
- Sheila
- Soledad
- Trista

Index

About the Author

JUSTIN CORD HAYES, author of *The Unexpected Evolution of Language* and coauthor of *The Big Book of Words You Should Know* and *Roget's Thesaurus of Words for Intellectuals*, is an experienced journalist and teacher. He was born in Memphis (the "Detroit of the South") and grew up in Knoxville, Tennessee. His name is not terrible. Justin is the fifty-ninth most popular name in the country; it derives from the Latin *iustis*, meaning just. Hayes is ranked 776 as a first name. It derives from a Gaelic surname, *O hAodha*, which means descendant of fire. Cord, on the other hand, isn't ranked. Supposedly, it's a diminutive of Conrad, but his folks got the name from the Cord, a short-lived automobile make with front-wheel drive and retractable headlights that they believed was ahead of its time.